From Cara

Impressions of Imagination:

Terra-Cotta Seattle

OPEN
OPEN
OPEN
4'-1"
12"
2'-0"
5'-0"
4'-0"
B
C
BRICK
LINE OF CONC.
3'-6"
3'-4"
9'-6"
45°
1'-7 3/4"

I m p r e s s i o n s

Impressions of Imagination:

Terra-Cotta Seattle

With an Introduction
by Robert Venturi

Allied Arts of Seattle, Inc.
107 South Main Street
Seattle, Washington 98104

I m a g i n a t i o n

Published 1986
Printed in U.S.A.
91 90 89 88 87 5 4 3 2 1

Library of Congress Cataloging-in-Publication Data
Main entry under title:
Impressions of Imagination.

1. Terra-cotta—Washington (State)—Seattle.
2. Decoration and ornament, Architectural—Washington (State)—Seattle. 3. Seattle (Wash.)—Buildings, structures, etc. I. Aldredge, Lydia. II. Allied Arts of Seattle, Inc.
NA3511.S52I45 1986 720′.9797′77 85-20138
ISBN 0-9615552-0-3

Table of Contents

Introduction

Robert Venturi

Opportunities abound for using terra-cotta for the sensual enrichment of architecture. It is a surface material for inside and out that promotes ornament—ornament involving color, pattern, and relief; ornament reinforcing structural or formal qualities; ornament as accent or delineation or as overall pattern. These decorative qualities can be more or less abstract or representational, conventional or original, geometrical or soft—the latter quality is especially natural to this material. Because of its easy repetitiveness and inherent refinement, terra-cotta can be a means of creating small-scale articulation as a counterpoint to the big size of many of our buildings today: it is a way to bring back "human scale" to our cities, as well as color and ornament.

Seattle is blessed with wonderful examples of terra-cotta used in a variety of ways, formal and symbolic, from the graceful and sophisticated classicism of the A. E. Doyle and Times Square Buildings to the exuberant whimsy of the Arctic Club and Coliseum Theater. It is the material of many of the Palazzo-like, ten- to twelve-story buildings of the early part of this century that have survived in downtown Seattle and contribute to its distinctive and pleasing scale.

The essays and photographs that follow celebrate this diversity. The essays as a collection cover many topics. Some delve into the works in terra-cotta of a particular designer while others concentrate on a specific period. Others look at regional aspects of terra-cotta or focus on its use on a particular building type. The photographs capture the sensual aspects of the material as words cannot. Together with the building inventory, the essays and photographs form a document that should prove valuable to both aficionado and layman.

It is to be hoped that these studies will create an awareness of terra-cotta and its importance and thus encourage both its preservation in old buildings and its use in new ones. In a period when architects and the public are rediscovering ornament and decoration in architecture, a beautiful publication like this is indeed timely.

Robert Venturi
August 28, 1985

***Olympic Tower Building** (cat. 71)*
Henry Bittman, Architect, c. 1929
Detail of Terra-Cotta ornament
Courtesy of Bittman, Vammen, Taylor PS
Because of its easy repetitiveness and inherent refinement terra-cotta can be a means of creating small scale articulation as a counterpoint to the big size of many of our buildings. . . .

Preface

Lydia S. Aldredge

Coliseum Theater
(cat. 60)
Both the old and the new are necessary for a rich urban context.

Generically, terra-cotta is an enriched molded clay block or brick. At the turn of this century in America, terra-cotta became popular for the cladding and ornamentation of structures. Its widespread application was based on several interrelated factors: the advent of structural steel frame construction, modern fireproofing requirements, waterproofing and cleaning considerations, the rising costs of ornamental stonework, and the material's extensive form and color possibilities. The years 1890-1940 marked the heyday of terra-cotta manufacture and installation. Many American cities experienced unprecedented growth during this period and thus contain extensive inventories of terra-cotta structures. On the west coast, Seattle, Portland, and San Francisco all possess rich and varied assemblages of terra-cotta architecture. San Francisco and Portland have recognized this architectural legacy with landmark designations, historic districts, and extensive surveys and documentary research. Until now, no comprehensive appraisal of Seattle's large inventory of terra-cotta has been completed.

Members of Allied Arts of Seattle, a local arts and urban design advocacy organization, became aware of Seattle's terra-cotta legacy during their years of participation in the design of a new downtown plan for the city of Seattle. During this planning process, Allied Arts members discovered that many of the terra-cotta structures included in this inventory contributed to the urban design features most valued by the organization and by members of the community: most of these terra-cotta buildings are scaled and oriented to enhance the downtown street environment; many create and reinforce the individual character of Seattle's distinct downtown neighborhoods; and several are irreplaceable set-pieces of public art in their totality and in their ornamental detail.

Seattle's continued growth and redevelopment have created a now familiar controversy: that of preservation of a historic architectural context versus new development with its promise of vitality and amenity. Both the old and the new are necessary for a rich urban context. The difficulty comes in determining the exact mix. The major purpose of this publication is to provide an overview of an identifiable inventory of historic structures so that development decisions are well integrated. Recognizing that many of the terra-cotta structures included in this inventory will disappear as the city matures, another aim is to create a record of Seattle's historic terra-cotta structures existing in 1985. Just as archival photographs establish an understanding of this city's history, so it is our intention that this publication will provide insight into Seattle's contemporary urban environment, by its focus on the significance of the city's terra-cotta architecture.

Coliseum Theater *(cat. 60)*

Asahel Curtis photograph

Courtesy of the Washington State Historical Society

Several are irreplaceable set-pieces of public art
in their totality and in their ornamental detail.

1 The History of American Terra-Cotta and its Local Manufacture

Mark Smith

Cobb Building *(cat. 68)*
Howell & Stokes, Architects, c. 1909
Terra-Cotta Indian Head Ornament
The Indian heads on the Cobb Building were modeled from Edward S. Curtis photographs of architectural sculpture by the New York firm, Rochette & Parzini.

The New York architectural critic, Herbert Crowley, on a 1912 western tour for the *Architectural Record,* informed his readers that almost all of Seattle's permanent buildings had been constructed during the past fifteen years and they were "fairly representative of the better American standards of commercial construction." This new architecture, which so rapidly and remarkably created new business districts for Seattle and many other American cities, was, as Louis Sullivan described, "that form of lofty construction called the modern office building."

The emergence of the skyscraper in the last quarter of the nineteenth century and its adoption as an accepted building type; its use of the new, fireproofed metal framing system; and the burgeoning growth of urban America all contributed to the full development of architectural glazed terra-cotta as a modern building material.

Prior to its adaptation to the tall building in the 1870s, terra-cotta, typically coated with a dull finish slip or painted to resemble brownstone, ornamented a small number of load-bearing masonry buildings of modest height. About 1840, terra-cotta produced in the Boston area was used limitedly in New England and in 1853 New York architect James Renwick substituted terra-cotta produced by a local sewer pipe manufacturer for cut stone on several buildings. However, stone cutters and builders unfamiliar with terra-cotta vigorously opposed it and temporarily prevented its further use.

Chicago was the first American city to build extensively with terra-cotta following the great fire of 1871 which demonstrated to the real-estate and building industries terra-cotta's fire-resistant qualities. As Chicago was being rebuilt with terra-cotta into a tall city, so Seattle would follow in 1889 after its own devastating fire and the resulting ordinance that required buildings within certain boundaries to be fireproof.

The skyscraper required a fireproof cladding that was lightweight, economically constructed in small pieces, and the surface of which could be artistically varied. While brick or stone masonry could be used to clad a building, the advantage of terra-cotta was its malleability, which allowed the architect to work with any number of ornamental forms and to use either solid color or polychrome. Frank Lloyd Wright observed that terra-cotta "takes the impression of human imagination .... It is in the architect's hand what wax is in the sculptor's hand."

In early skyscraper construction, hollow clay tile brick was used both to cover the steel frame and for the floor construction, while the exterior was clad entirely in terra-cotta or mixed ornamentally with masonry. The weight of the cladding — terra-cotta was about 70 pounds per cubic foot as compared to 170 pounds for the same volume of granite — was carried by the metal frame.

A mold for a particular piece of terra-cotta could be used to produce many duplicates of the piece, keeping the unit cost economical. Many of the ornamental and flat ashlar pieces were standard forms that the manufacturers kept in stock and could produce quickly and easily. However, most of the terra-cotta for Seattle's buildings was custom-designed.

Cobb Building *(cat. 68)*
Asahel Curtis photograph
Courtesy of the Washington State Historical Society
Frank Lloyd Wright observed that terra-cotta "takes the impression of imagination ... it is in the architect's hand what wax is in the sculptor's hand."

Terra-Cotta Corinthian capitol

Courtesy of R. F. McCann, Priteca's file

An example of the high art obtained by the clay workers' handicraft.

The modelers employed by the terra-cotta companies were for the most part born and trained in Europe. The Indian heads on the Cobb Building, for instance, were modeled from Edward S. Curtis photographs by the New York architectural sculpture firm of Rochette & Parzini. Both men had studied at the Ecole des Beaux Arts in Paris.

The initial heavy demand was on local brick manufacturers, but four firms soon dominated the production of architectural terra-cotta for Seattle buildings: the Puget Sound Fire Clay Company, the Northern Clay Company, the Spokane-based Washington Brick, Lime, & Sewer Pipe Company and the Gladding-McBean Company of Lincoln City, California.

The Puget Sound Fire Clay Company was organized in 1882 with its office and yard at the corner of First Avenue and Jackson Street and its works near Van Asselt, the present site of the Boeing Airplane Company's administration building. The plant had a labor force of thirty men and included two small kilns; sewer pipe was its principal product. The company had financial difficulties with Arthur A. Denny as a major creditor. Denny took over the company and its debts and on April 1, 1892, the Denny Clay Company began operation. By 1900 the quality of its product established a market for the company not only in Washington but also in other Pacific Coast states, Alaska, and foreign countries. It purchased large land areas near Black Diamond and Taylor, thirty-five miles from Seattle on the Columbia & Puget Sound Railroad. Extensive clay and coal mines were opened at Taylor and a large plant was constructed. The Denny-Renton Clay & Coal Company was incorporated in 1905, combining the Denny Clay Company and the Renton Clay Company. Terra-cotta for the King County Courthouse, the Arctic Building, and the Times Building was produced by Denny-Renton.

The Northern Clay Company, organized in 1900 at Auburn, dug its clay from fifty acres of company property along the Green River about eight miles north of the plant. The clay was hauled by wagons to the factory, which consisted of three terra-cotta kilns and one fire brick kiln, along with other buildings for designing, molding and drying terra-cotta.

The Coliseum Theatre and the Washington Securities Building were clad in the Northern Clay Company's white satin-finished glazed terra-cotta; the Natatorium's ivory white terra-cotta, with the ornamentation on the pilasters and lower portions of the building highlighted by a background of golden yellow and green dolphins above the cornice, was also furnished by the company. Five hundred different shapes and sizes were used and the number of pieces totaled over 7,850. The 1920 terra-cotta contracts for the ten-story Telephone Building and the Washington Mutual Savings Bank Building were won by the company for a combined amount of approximately $50,000. Other buildings using Northern Clay's terra-cotta were the Joshua Green Building, the Securities Building, the Pantages Theatre, and Frederick & Nelson Department Store.

The Washington Brick, Lime, & Sewer Pipe Company's works at Clayton near Spokane were typical for a large terra-cotta manufacturing firm. The main works were housed in a four-story brick building 80 x 160 feet with auxiliary fitting sheds 400 x 30 feet along the sides. Nine down-draft muffled kilns fired the terra-cotta and the monthly production was about 450 tons.

The Gladding-McBean Company was the preeminent producer of terra-cotta in California and responsible for some of the finest work in the country. Many buildings in Seattle were supplied with terra-cotta by Gladding, McBean, including the Smith Tower, the Pioneer Building, and the Federal Office Building.

The industry promoted the use of terra-cotta through advertising, special exhibitions, and the extolling of the material by writers in architectural and building trade journals. The Denny-Renton Clay & Coal Company's exhibit at the 1909 Alaska-Yukon Pacific Exposition skillfully displayed its products under a four-column, canopied brick and terra-cotta pavilion. The columns that supported the roof of the pavilion were of white pressed brick surmounted with capitals of terra-cotta. Above the capitals were a cornice and frieze of multicolored brick. A reporter for a trade journal said, "this display may

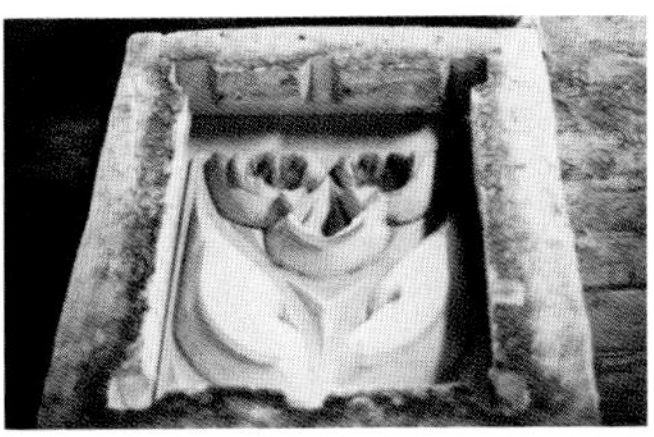

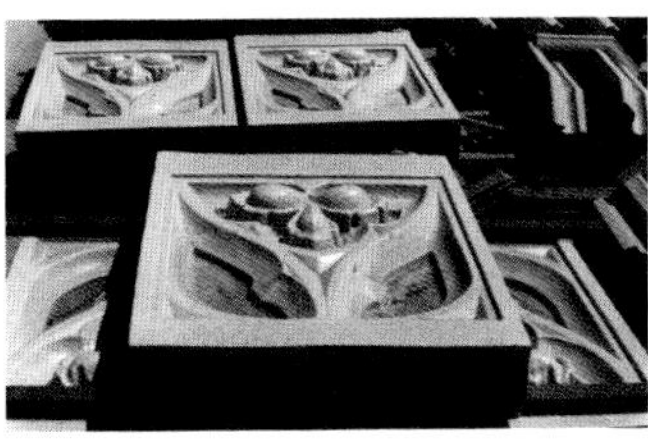

Terra-Cotta Mould

Courtesy of Gladding-McBean

Each mould had a four-inch-thick wall and was held together by metal straps. Clay was hand pressed into it to a depth of several inches and webs were built across the back to provide additional strength with minimal added weight.

well be considered as an exemplification of the high art obtained by the clay-worker's handicraft, and as such it is distinctive and representative."

Three years later, during the 1912 Potlatch Week celebration, the company entered a float in the Industrial Parade on Second Avenue. The Denny-Renton section was led by the Dentonians, the executives of the company, and was followed by the float carrying a brick kiln with a brick smokestack and smoke rolling out of it. The queen of the Denny-Renton sat on her throne and in front of her were two clay modelers at work modeling a Potlatch bug out of clay. Two pages on the float threw out souvenir terra-cotta match safes to the crowd. Five hundred persons represented the company in the various sections of its contingent. Each man in the march was dressed in uniform with a white military coat bearing the name, Denny-Renton, over the left pocket and a hat of imitation red brick on his head. Signs along the route indicated that Denny-Renton made fifty-eight million paving bricks annually, was the largest manufacturing concern in the state operating six clay factories, and employed 950 men with a payroll of $1.5 million.

Terra-Cotta Rosette and Acanthus leaf Rinceau

Courtesy of R. F. McCann, Priteca's file

The Washington Brick, Lime and Sewer Pipe Company's works... were typical for a large terra-cotta manufacturing firm.

After purchasing the Northern Clay Company in 1925 and merging with the Denny-Renton Clay & Coal Company in the same year, Gladding, McBean became one of the largest producers of terra-cotta in the country. The company had offices in the west, midwest, and Hawaii, and continued to provide substantial amounts of terra-cotta to the building industry. One of its product developments in the 1920s, terra-cotta veneer, was used extensively in Art Deco and Moderne buildings of the period, including the Woolworth store on Third Avenue.

The manufacturing process for terra-cotta involved the following procedures: the calculation of quantities from the architect's plans; the development of working drawings and full-size detail drawings showing the size and layout of all pieces; the preparation of the clay stock; the model and mold making; the pressing of the terra-cotta pieces and surface finishing, if required; drying; the preparation and application of colors and glazes; the lengthy firing of the pieces; and the fitting of the pieces after firing to ensure correct alignment and size.

The fine grade clay used for terra-cotta was plastic, yet capable of standing up to the firing. Grog, a previously fired, finely ground clay, was mixed with the raw, dried clay. A pugmill blended the wetted clay mixture to the right consistency and the resulting clay body was aged for a day or more. The models for the pieces were constructed with a combination of plaster for the body of the piece and clay for the details. The model allowed for the shrinkage of the clay during firing, usually about five to seven percent. Photographs of completed models were sent to the architect for approval prior to making the molds.

Molds were created by pouring liquid plaster over a completed model. The number of parts for a mold varied with the size and complexity of the design. The thickness of the walls of the mold was about four inches and the mold was held together by metal straps. The clay was hand-pressed into the mold several inches thick and webs were built across the back to the full depth of the mold in order to provide additional strength with minimal added weight. Holes for anchoring the pieces to the building with metal ties were also formed at this time. Certain profile shapes and terra-cotta veneer were produced by forcing wet clay through a steel die in an extruder and cutting it to the desired length. This process was introduced after 1900. The clay remained in the mold for a few hours and was then laid on racks for final surface finishing and a day of drying. The dried pieces were taken from the pressing area to the glazing room where they received a spray of slip undercoat and a glaze coat that could be in a range of colors and finishes: from white to polychrome and shiny to matte in a fine, mottled, or speckled pattern. Stone could easily be imitated with the glazed finish.

After the glazes were dry, the pieces were loaded into the kilns, slow-fired for several days, and fired at 2000 degrees for three to four days. The cooling of the kiln took two to three days, after which the pieces were checked for alignment, cracking and other defects. They were then trimmed before delivery to the job site.

By 1930 the demand for terra-cotta had started to decline because of rising production costs, the worsening of the Depression, and changing tastes in materials and architectural styles. The 1930s and 1940s saw the Woolworth store as the only new building constructed in downtown Seattle using terra-cotta. Gladding, McBean eventually closed its Auburn and Van Asselt terra-cotta works and consolidated operations in Renton. The Taylor coal and clay mines and the town were condemned by the Seattle Water Department in order to include the area inside an expanded watershed. The company built new offices and a warehouse on Elliott Avenue in 1954. Its new marketing emphasis was on face brick, ceramic veneer, and glazed masonry units. Gladding, McBean presently has only the Lincoln, California, plant and is one of only two or three remaining active terra-cotta manufacturers in the country.

The terra-cotta era was over, a long way from its eminent representation by Denny-Renton as the highlight of Seattle's boisterous summer celebration up its most urbane avenue, and proudly recalled by a ceramic engineer of the times: "We need not dwell on the many beautiful designs of buildings which are faced with terra-cotta. Every large business center of our cities stands as a monument for the terra-cotta industry."

Terra-Cotta Swagged Bracket
Courtesy of R. F. McCann, Priteca's file

Securities Building *(cat. 96)*
John Graham, Sr.; Frank Allen, Architects, c. 1912/1915
The Coliseum Theater and the Washington Securities Building were clad in the Northern Clay Company's white, satin-finish, glazed terra-cotta.

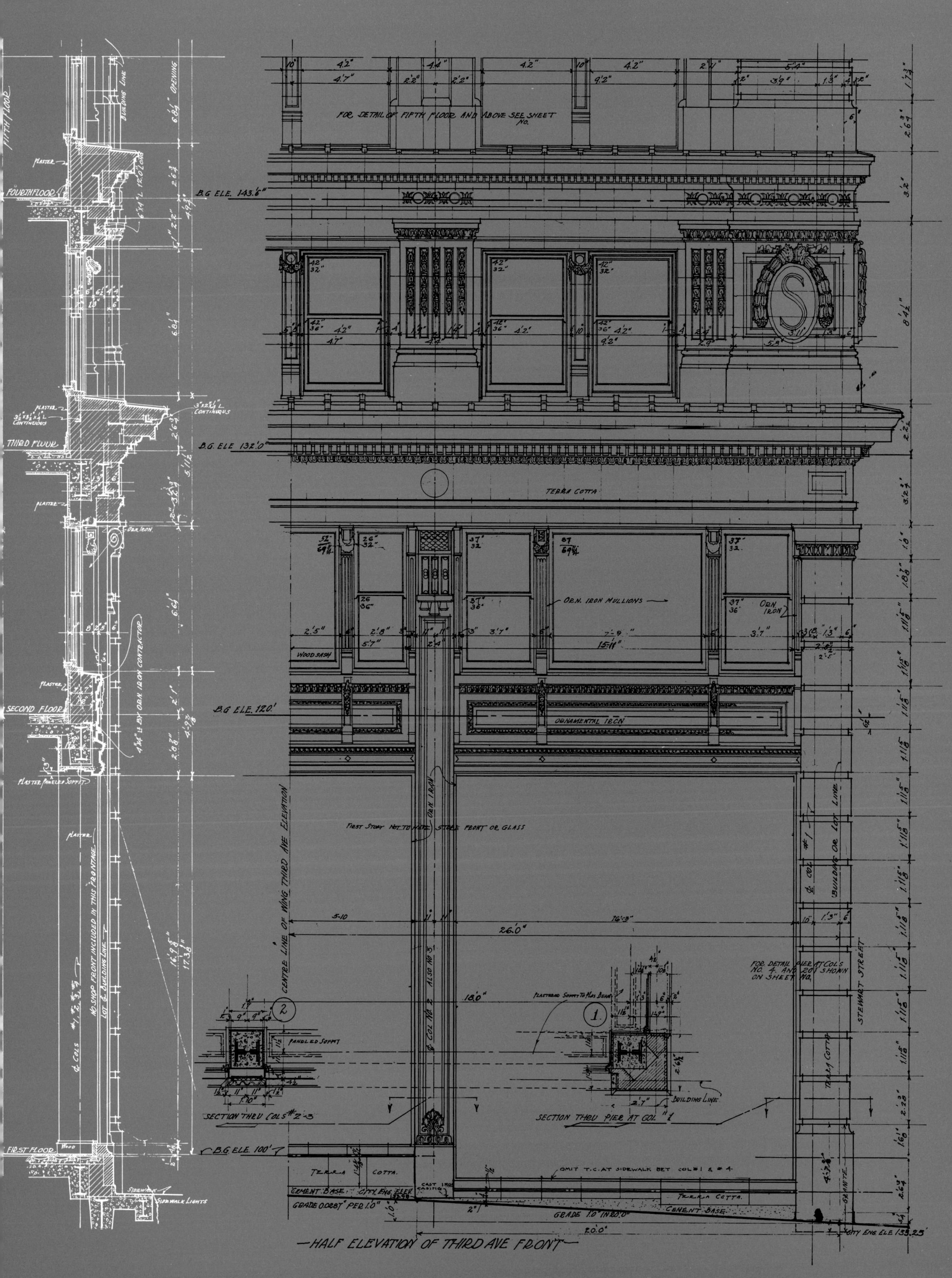

FIFTH FLOOR
FOURTH FLOOR
THIRD FLOOR
SECOND FLOOR
FIRST FLOOR
PLASTER
BUILDING LINE
PLASTER PANELED SOFFIT
NO SHOP FRONT INCLUDED IN THIS FRONTAGE
SIDEWALK LIGHTS
B.G. ELE. 143.6"
B.G. ELE. 132.0"
B.G. ELE. 120.0'
B.G. ELE. 100'
FOR DETAIL OF FIFTH FLOOR AND ABOVE SEE SHEET NO.
TERRA COTTA
ORN. IRON MULLIONS
WOOD SASH
ORNAMENTAL IRON
ORN. IRON
FIRST STORY NOT TO HAVE STORE FRONT OR GLASS
CENTRE LINE OF WING THIRD AVE ELEVATION
BUILDING OR LOT LINE
FOR DETAIL PIER AT COLS NO. 4 AND 20 SHOWN ON SHEET NO.
STEWART STREET
PLASTERED SOFFIT TO MAS. BEAM
PANELED SOFFIT
SECTION THRU COLS #2-3
SECTION THRU PIER AT COL. #1
OMIT T.C. AT SIDEWALK BET. COL #1 & #4
CEMENT BASE
GRADE 1.0" IN 20.0"
GRANITE
CITY ENG. ELE. 133.23
26.0"
20.0"
HALF ELEVATION OF THIRD AVE FRONT

2 Terra-Cotta Clad and Ornamented Buildings in Seattle

Earl Layman and Matthew Lampe

***Dexter Horton Building, Alaska Building, and the Smith Tower** (cat. 24, 25, 27)*

The development of the skyscraper led to an explosion in the use of terra-cotta as a major material both to partially clad structures and to provide rich ornament.

Terra-cotta appeared as a medium for architectural ornamentation at the turn of the century in Seattle. Before its ascendancy as a cladding material, terra-cotta became an alternative to carved stone and pressed metal as a vehicle for ornament and detail. Terra-cotta detailing was used from the 1890s through the 1930s, appearing in the styles of the *Beaux Arts, Art Deco* and *Moderne*.

An early extant example of terra-cotta-ornamented architecture was designed by Bebb & Mendel as a six-story business building in 1901 for Haim and Schultz. This building, in the Pioneer Square Historic District and adjacent to the better known Alaska Building is now known as the Corona Hotel. The composition, color, and detailing are reminiscent of the work of Louis Sullivan. Its detailing makes extensive use of reddish, unglazed terra-cotta panels on the first floor, and in the upper level friezes and cornice, which display elaborate floral patterns.

The development of the skyscraper led to an explosion in the use of terra-cotta as a major material both to partially clad structures and to provide rich ornament. The skyscraper, or as Louis Sullivan called it, "the tall building triumphant," was born in Chicago little more than a century ago. There were several concurrent reasons for the creation of the skyscraper: the perfection of the Bessemer process for fabricating structural steel; the invention of the electric elevator; and the rapid, industrialized growth of cities, causing tremendous increases in land values and concentration of people and functions.

Although Seattle at the turn of the century was little more than a rough and ready small, frontier town, and, until the gold rushes, was competing economically with such rivals as Port Townsend and Tacoma, the earliest skyscrapers here appeared in the first fifteen years of the twentieth century. The first was the Alaska Building on Second Avenue. The second was the Hoge Building at the northwest corner of the same intersection. And the third was the Smith Tower, said to be the tallest building west of the Mississippi until after World War II. They all demonstrated the advantages and the excitement of steel-cage construction, combined with new methods of sheathing these structures. Very often the earliest skyscrapers in the Middle West necessarily combined cast iron, wrought iron, and early steel with masonry-bearing walls, both inside and outside. No engineering tables, handbooks, or body of experience existed to aid these new experiments. An example of this in Seattle is the Pioneer Building at First Avenue and Yesler Way, which was completed spasmodically following the 1889 Great Fire. This building contains within it a combination of structural steel, structural cast iron, and structural wood. Still it is dependent on masonry walls to provide the external and some internal vertical stability.

When the Alaska Building was created just a few years later, in 1903, it was tall enough to demand a different method of structure and sheathing. The same requirements were met for the Northern Securities Building in 1906 and the Hoge Building in 1911. In these two cases we see a combination of a brick skin and lavish use of terra-cotta decorative elements: pilasters, capitals, window surrounds, cornices, orna-

***Arctic Club** (cat. 21)*

A. Warren Gould, Architect, c. 1914/1917

Detail of walrus head ornament. A modest high-rise office building incorporating more colored terra-cotta than most of the other buildings.

The Rhodes Building
(demolished)

Asahel Curtis photograph Courtesy of the Washington State Historical Society

Despite the loss of some of Seattle's finer examples, terra-cotta remains a source of the splendor, richness and architectural variety that contribute to Seattle's vibrant urban environment.

ment. But when the Smith Tower was conceived, the technology employed on these two previous skyscrapers was no longer adequate and this building was sheathed and ornamented entirely in terra-cotta, and rose to a height of approximately forty-two stories. It expresses its skeletal structure well, since the sheathing occurs only over major structural elements, both vertical and horizontal.

Following the completion of the Smith Tower in 1914, the use of the new technology to produce a lightweight, weatherproof skin which could easily be attached to the structural steel frame of buildings became very prevalent in Seattle. This book attests that most of the buildings built for three decades thereafter in the downtown employed this method to varying degrees.

Another example of a modest highrise office building employing terra-cotta is the Arctic Building on Third Avenue, which incorporates more color than most of the other buildings. One of the finest examples of a terra-cotta clad, steel-framed office building is the Shafer at Sixth and Pine. It incorporates a little Gothic ornament in the spandrels, the shaping of some of the window surrounds, and in the topmost finials of the facades, but basically it is reduced to pure bones and skin and expresses those components better than many of our current glass-sheathed buildings which deny their underlying structures. Other significant highrise, fully-clad buildings include the Joshua Green, the Ligget, and the Republic Buildings.

Another advantage of terra-cotta was its plastic nature which made it possible to develop any kind of ornament in any style or mode at a reasonable cost. Most of the terra-cotta clad and ornamented buildings were designed during the heyday of *beaux-arts* architectural education, which emphasized the use of historic styles and classical motifs. The use of terra-cotta made feasible the inclusion of symbols of instant culture whether for commercial, residential, religious, educational, industrial, recreational, or cultural purposes. In most cases, however, the potential variations of style may be observed in such disparate side-by-side examples as the Sheridan Apartments and the Griffin Business College, at 2011 and 2004 Fifth Avenue respectively. The first is neo-classical/Renaissance revival architecture, and the second is modified Gothic.

North and east of the city's first business district—Pioneer Square—and the early developments along Second Avenue, there arose a new "city within a city" on the original site of the University of Washington. The University's trustees commissioned outstanding New York architects to plan this development, which was never completely finished. Its first buildings included the recently refurbished Olympic Hotel, the Cobb Building, and the recently demolished White Henry Stuart Building, Metropolitan Theatre, Metropolitan garage, and other structures. On all these buildings the designers used generous amounts of terra-cotta ornament and sheathing at the lower and crowning stories, with light tan brick sheathing between. Ornament included rich bracketry, pedimented windows, cartouches, cornices, pilasters and capitals, and, perhaps most impressively on the Cobb and White Henry Stuart Buildings, large and fearsome Indian heads which made obeisance to the local indigenous culture.

Terra-cotta ornament graced more than the period's dominant office and business structures. The material was found on a variety of downtown buildings, including warehouse and retail buildings, hotels and apartments. The dominant application of the material was to clad the street-level facades to provide a more elegant contact with pedestrians. Buildings were also frequently crowned with terra-cotta tile and ornamental details to add style and unique presence. The Terminal Sales Building, designed by Henry Bittman and constructed in 1923 for the Pacific Warehouse Company, demonstrates the fanciful use of terra-cotta in a Tudor arch, on turret caps, on pilasters, shields and in a grape and floral design motif. This motif is continued above the elaborately clad two-story base with the use of terra-cotta spandrels and rosettes. The building is crowned with terra-cotta parapets with alternating indentations, creating the illusion of medieval battlements.

Examples of other significant lowrise structures with complete terra-cotta sheathing include the former Natatorium at First and Bell, the Coliseum Theatre at Fifth and Pike, the Decatur Building, and portions of the now demolished Pilgrim Congregational Church, whose terra-cotta columns now stand alone overlooking the freeway at Pike and Boren.

Downtown residential structures built during the early part of this century also provide evidence of the ornamental value of terra-cotta. Hotels such as the New Washington, Frye, Mayflower, Camlin, and Roosevelt, and apartment houses such as the McKay, Oxford, and Palladian all use terra-cotta to provide decorative accents to their structures. The New Washington Hotel, built in 1906 and among the first of the Regrade buildings, is typical of these residential structures with its extensive use of terra-cotta elements to define the street facades and entrances, and emphasize the windows of the major public spaces.

Throughout downtown Seattle, significant buildings built prior to the Great Depression made extensive use of terra-cotta as a medium for ornamentation. Segments of the material, in many colors, glazed and unglazed, provide a myriad of architectural detail, from plain wall surfaces and repetitive elements to elaborate spandrels and cornices, with which the architects, artists and artisans of the day could create fanciful and unique buildings. Despite the loss of some of Seattle's finer examples, terra-cotta is a distinguishing feature of many of the first buildings constructed during the development of downtown Seattle, and remains a source of the splendor, richness and architectural variety that contribute to Seattle's vibrant architectural and urban environment.

2005
5th AVE.

Griffin Business College *(cat. 88)*
Frank H. Fowler, Architect, c. 1927
An example of the modified gothic style which once rivaled the neo-classical in popularity.

Hoge Building *(cat. 31)*
Bebb & Mendel, Architects, c. 1911
We see a combination of a brick skin and lavish use of terra-cotta decorative elements: pilasters, capitals, window surrounds, cornices, ornament.

Downtown Mini-Warehouse *(cat. 97)*
Henry Bittman, Architect, c. 1928
The material was found on a variety of downtown buildings including warehouse and retail buildings, hotels and apartments.

Peoples National Bank *(cat. 98)*
Charles Haynes, Architect, c. 1921
The use of terra-cotta made feasible the inclusion of symbols of instant culture. . .

3 The Ornament of Terra-Cotta

Karl Kotas

Terra-Cotta Cartouche
Courtesy of R. F. McCann, Priteca's file

Bethel Pentecostal Temple *(cat. 107)*
B. Marcus Priteca, Architect, c. 1916
Terra-Cotta Cartouche
What other building material or architectural style is as hospitable to the neon razzmatazz, the hand scrawled signage...?

The first terra-cotta was of course pottery and it is fitting that some of the most familiar motifs in our survey appeared as painted bands on ancient Greek vases before becoming sculptured ornaments on stone temples. While some of these forms began as decoration, such as fretwork, anthemions, guilloche and scrolls, many others derive from ancient religious rites. The first Greek temples were built of wood and tile with pitched roofs and porches upheld by log beams. On festival days garlands of flowers, fruit and aromatic leaves, bound in ribbons, were hung between the skulls of oxen sacrificed upon the altars. In time, the log beams became stone columns and the ox skulls and garlands became sculptured borders of bucraniums and festoons as the classical orders were developed. In Roman times, the orders were adapted to the cladding of the massive buildings of rubble-bearing wall construction, and columns became pilasters. What was structure in one became ornament in another.

With the fall of Rome and the subsequent decentralization of knowledge and culture during the Middle Ages, the classical orders were replaced by a new religious architecture in Western Europe—the Gothic style. Heavenward soared the spire and arch, tracery and buttress, as if to catch the soul's flight in stone. Also medieval, the Romanesque style derived from classic sources in Byzantium, transmitted from the Eastern Roman Empire to trading partners in Italian city states. This Romanesque style came to symbolize spiritual inspiration while it retained the signs of pagan religions as ornamental motifs.

The institution of heraldry in the Middle Ages provided another source of ornament. A largely illiterate warrior class devised a symbol system with painted shields and hung the shields on the walls of their fortresses. As nobility became more a matter of material wealth than martial valor, the shields became the blank ovals of noncombatants (such as highborn churchmen), superimposed upon scrolled parchment, signifying the patents of nobility granted to the new class of merchant princes. Thus the coats of arms hung on castle walls became stone cartouches on the cornices of chateaux. Similarly, the structural inventions of the Gothic cathedrals became decorative cladding on buildings in subsequent eras.

By Victorian times the use of ornament was rampant. Buildings, tools, furniture and machinery were festooned with paradigms lost to the pawnshops of history. Vines and foliage entwined about curling scrolls, mythic beasts leapt, crawled, flew and lay atop armoires and armories. It was in reaction to this seeming Baroque excess that the apostles of Modernism railed against ornament, presenting us with the undecorated slabs of glass and steel that now tower over the masonry and terra-cotta structures which graced our perhaps more exuberant years before and just after World War I.

The days of Gothic and Classical revival are over and it is far from certain that the buildings we still see from this era will last much longer; but one can still walk the streets of Seattle and see some of the history of Western architecture and culture recapitulated on the sides of the terra-cotta office buildings that are, surprisingly, still abundant.

Terra-Cotta Niche
Courtesy of R. F. McCann, Priteca's file

GLADD
1 2 3
14

4 A Photographer's Climb to Get Close to the Terra-Cotta on the Canyon of Dreams

Paul Dorpat

***Smith Tower** (cat. 27)*
Gaggin & Gaggin, Architects, c. 1912
Will enlarging or getting closer to the wall of a modern curtain glass tower lead you to such delights?

It is an odd photograph of the Smith Tower that does not concentrate on the tower. This portrait of L.C Smith's monument to himself looks down on its bottom half only, from the roof of the Frye Hotel. The peculiar angle was the choice of a now unknown photographer who, judging from the few hundred dusty negatives that survive him, had not developed an interest in cityscapes. Most of his subjects were of family, friends and lovers (I presume), artfully arranged on front porches, beside waterfalls or within the shelter of rhododendrons.

In this pile of negatives there's also a self-portrait of the smiling amateur pulling a string that loops to his camera. And he was a good photographer; by that I mean his negatives are usually in focus, his compositions pleasing and his subjects often exciting. But what motivated this good-natured snap-shooter, who rarely ever took his camera downtown, to scramble onto a roof for this oddly decapitated record of the Smith Tower's terra-cotta face, shot at the level of its fourteenth story?

Fourteen stories was "about the right height" L.C. Smith and James D. Hoge agreed for the new skyscrapers they planned to develop within two blocks of one another at the southern end of Second Avenue. While visiting the 1909 Alaska Yukon and Pacific Exposition in Seattle, they met and sized each other up. What then motivated Hoge in 1911 to raise his tower eighteen stories and soon after Smith his to forty-two, is much easier to understand than the photographer's will to climb to the roof.

Second Avenue by 1909 was already the city's cosmopolitan canyon with polished and well-fit sides crafted from recalcitrant substances like stone and willing ones like terra-cotta. These were materials on which one could carve out ornament—if one were skilled. So regardless of your name, Smith or Hoge, your fortune, made in typewriters or real estate, or how monumental your amibition or kitschy your taste, if you were going to build on Second Avenue you had a civic responsibility that was prescribed by the example of these materials. Of course at that time there was no rule about how high you could take your building.

***Alaska Building** (cat. 25)*
Eames & Young, Architects, c. 1904
Second Avenue Entry
By 1909, Second Avenue was the city's cosmopolitan canyon with polished and well-fitted sides crafted from recalcitrant substances like stone and willing ones like terra-cotta.

***Lowman Building** (cat. 32)*
Heide & deNeuf, Architects, c. 1905
The Pioneer Square Skyline
L.C. Smith would agree to raise the tallest building west of New York in the old part of town.

Old Timers Cafe

***Smith Tower** (cat. 27)*
Construction Photograph, c. 1911

Potlatch Parade
Northern view of the 1913 parade from a Spring Street rooftop.

Potlatch Parade
Southern view of the parade down the Second Avenue canyon.

Seattle was exploding then, growing so fast that it had lost its center. Anxious officials and superstitious speculators went searching for the city's center, earnestly mud-wrestling with the topography, forcing regrades on its rolling streets and plump little hills. Denny Hill was washed away because it was claimed to "inhibit the natural northerly expansion of the city." In the process much mud spattered the terra-cotta as they splashed about searching for the main chance and digging for the "highest and best use."

Of course, this hunt for a civic center was more often than not a desire to be the center. For instance, before L.C. Smith would agree to raise the tallest building west of New York in the old part of town and name it after himself, he extracted from the city a promise that it would not move city hall north to the new part of town.

But Second Avenue was already above and beyond this anxiety, for the "canyon" ran between the old and new parts of town. It was in fact an unrolled city center extending twelve blocks from the curve at Yesler Way to the curve at Stewart Street. Through the first twenty years of this century this stretch was a cosmopolitan answer to the provincial passion for another hot spot like the old Pioneer Place. Second Avenue was not a planned boulevard. Its unity derived from desires more diverse than schematic.

But why was the photographer on the roof? The odd-sized negative ($3\frac{1}{4}$ x $5\frac{1}{2}$ inches) has not been cropped in this printing, but its focus is sharp and it could have been cropped. With an enlarger we might move straight on to the "pure white ornamental terra-cotta" at the fourteenth floor, enjoy its decorative details and ornamental surprises, and cross the line where the tiles meet the bronze window sash and frames. Will enlarging or getting close to the wall of a modern glass curtain tower lead you into such delights?

The Smith Tower was dedicated on July 4, 1914. This photograph was probably shot the preceding winter, for the afternoon sun throws long shadows. In this light the Lilliputian figures on the street and sidewalk below receive such a sculptured dignity that they are the equal of the monumental white mass that rises above them. Perhaps this is the odd consequence, if not motive, of the photographer's climb, that his scene captures Smith's symbol in an intimate light standing as part of a human group, joining in a conversation with the men and women on the street and beside it. Buildings do not always speak for their builders.

For a quarter of a century the Second Avenue canyon was Seattle's parade route. The Golden Potlatch was the city's first official summer festival. The two views included here of the 1913 Potlach parade look north and south on Second Avenue from a rooftop at Spring Street. In between these celebrations the avenue was itself a parade. The pedestrian could perambulate along this civilized strip and enjoy the many urbane touches. The avenue's many terra-cotta sides and ornaments were essential to this enjoyment. The skin of this ancient clay, whether rough or glazed, invited the touch, for others' hands were behind it. It was this well-crafted and slow-cooked cover that hung a lightweight intimacy on cold structural steel and gave a frame "nobility without intimidation."

And it could also send a photographer to the top of one skyscraper in a successful attempt to get close to the terra-cotta of another.

***Smith Tower** (cat. 27)*
Asahel Curtis photograph
Courtesy of the Washington State Historical Society
Much mud splattered the terra-cotta as they splashed about searching for the main chance and the "highest and best use."

RAINIER
BEER
Curtis © 1912
28684

5 Seattle in Search of Symbolic Self-Expression: The Architecture of Bebb and Gould

T. William Booth

Puget Sound Mill Co. *(cat. 35)*
Bebb & Gould, Architects, c. 1924
Spring Street Entrance Archway
Courtesy of Mrs. Anne Gould Hauberg
The architectural expression of Seattle's noble aspirations and powerful ambitions.

Charles H. Bebb (1856-1942), an expatriate Englishman, and Carl F. Gould (1873-1939), a native New Yorker, were patrician transplants to Seattle, at the turn of the century a frontier town undergoing rapid transformation into a major Pacific-coastal metropolis. It was a city in search of symbolic expression for its newly attained wealth and success. More recently, the international mark of urban sophistication and achievement has been the glass- and granite-sheathed office tower. In the first decade of the twentieth century the architecture signifying civic pride and commercial success was an eclectic historical selection executed in stone, masonry, and terra-cotta.

Bebb and Gould were designers whose professional experience prepared them for the challenge of constructing major structures for a new city. We see today a distillation of their international experience: their strolls on the Parisian boulevards, their study of imperial Roman ruins, and their analysis of the Chicago steel-frame office tower. From these world centers each came to Seattle for brief visits and returned to express through their architecture this city's noble aspirations and powerful ambitions.

Charles H. Bebb arrived in Seattle in 1890 on assignment from the Chicago architectural firm of Adler & Sullivan to supervise the erection of a steel-frame office building on Second Avenue. Bebb's chosen profession, civil engineering, had brought him far from his genteel childhood in Surrey, England, and his studies at the University of Lausanne, Switzerland, at King's College, and at The School of Mines in London. Pursuing a civil engineering career, Bebb had traveled to South Africa to work for five years on the Cape Town/Kimberly Railroad and then to Chicago in 1882 to secure a position with the Illinois Central Railroad. However, upon arriving in Chicago, Bebb accepted an offer from the Illinois Terra-Cotta Lumber Company, a leading terra-cotta manufacturer, and began his professional education as a construction engineer and architect. At this time the primary use of terra-cotta was in the fireproofing of Chicago's newly invented and evolving steel-frame structures. His new position gained Bebb expertise with the material and with the requirements of the Chicago frame building. He formed professional relationships with the architects of these buildings and eventually joined the office of Adler & Sullivan as a supervising architect. Employed in the most acclaimed architectural office of that era, Bebb gained invaluable experience detailing Sullivan's ornamental designs in architectural terra-cotta. He also supervised the construction of several major civic commissions, including the Chicago Auditorium Building. As one of Adler & Sullivan's supervising architects, Bebb arrived in Seattle only to see the projected work evaporate when its financing dissolved in a bank failure. Bebb returned to Adler & Sullivan's office in Chicago, but moved permanently to Seattle a few months later. Once again, Bebb's employer was a terra-cotta manufacturer, the Denny Clay Company located in Renton, Washington. He engineered terra-cotta projects for five years for this concern. In 1898, at the age of forty-two, Bebb

Watermark Tower *(cat. 35)*
Renovation and Addition, The Bumgardner Architects, c. 1983
Beaux-arts principles at work: the vocabulary of classical forms and historical culture incorporated in the design of modern building types.

formed an architectural practice. Working initially with the architect Mendel, Bebb's practice designed several commercial structures ornamented with terra-cotta. The earliest of these, the Corona Hotel of 1903, exhibits Bebb's stylistic debt to Sullivan with its horizontal facade organization and its sinuous floral ornamentation in unglazed terra-cotta. Bebb & Mendel's later buildings, the Frye Hotel and the Hoge Building, were less derivative and more historicist in their ornamentation.

Carl F. Gould joined his architectural practice with that of Charles Bebb in 1914 to produce structure that would stand as a symbol of cultural refinement. If Charles Bebb was the consummate technician, Carl Gould was an artistically gifted architect with extensive archeological and historical knowledge. He was born in Manhattan in 1873 to a family tracing its New York lineage to the early seventeenth century and to American Revolutionary War generals. The artists John Singer Sargent and William Merritt Chase provide vivid portraits of Gould's class of New Yorker. New York was a rich cultural milieu, filled with opportunities for artistic inspiration and intellectual enlightenment. Carl Gould appears to have seized and savored these opportunities. He graduated from the exclusive Phillips Exeter Academy in 1894 and obtained a Bachelor of Arts degree from Harvard University in 1898. Gould's education culminated in a journey to Paris in 1899 to study at the Ecole des Beaux Arts.

At this time the Ecole des Beaux Arts was the preeminent institution for architectural instruction in the world. It was a mecca for American architects whose graduates include William Morris Hunt, H.H. Richardson, Charles F. McKim, and Bernard Maybeck. Balancing design, architectural history, construction technology, and mathematics, the Ecole's curriculum remains the fundamental format for architectural education to this day. There, Gould was indoctrinated with an architectural design theory based on the universal principles of scale, proportion, and organization as expressed in classical culture. Instruction incorporated the vocabulary of classical forms and historical culture in the design of modern building types accommodating new functions. Historical reference and association were accomplished in the design of ornamentation based on the archeological discoveries of the previous century.

The majority of an Ecole student's instruction in this design philosophy occurred in the atelier of an academician. Gould was a gifted student with Victor Laloux, an elegant studio instructor popular with American students. Under Laloux's tutelage Gould won five academy medals and exhibited his designs in the Paris Salon of 1902. During this time Gould traveled to Italy, England, and throughout France recording in ink and watercolor wash the ruins of classical culture and the monuments of Western European civilization. Despite his evident artistic abilities, Gould was not able to complete his studies at the Ecole: he could not master the mathematical section of the curriculum.

In 1903 Gould returned to New York to work with that city's most celebrated architectural office, McKim Meade & White. Here he gained practical experience in the design of neo-classical facades and hierarchic plans for railway terminuses and museum collections. Gould became familiar with terra-cotta ornamentation and cladding in his work on the Pennsylvania Station and Brooklyn Museum projects. He grew more accomplished with this style and building material working with other Beaux Arts-trained firms, Carrere & Hastings and George B. Post.

However, Carl Gould, like Charles Bebb, was not content to remain an apprentice to genius. Chance and circumstance brought Gould to Seattle in 1908. While on board a train, touring the Pacific coast for relaxation after a frenzied year of New York architectural practice, Gould became seriously ill with appendicitis. He remained in Seattle for several months recuperating from this illness in the home of old acquaintances from his days at Harvard. Perhaps Seattle enchanted this seasoned traveler with its panoramic vistas, its economic vitality and its cultural ambitions, just as it enchants newcomers today. Shortly after this experience Gould returned to Seattle to establish an architectural practice.

Bebb and Gould's fruitful collaboration began in 1914 with the design of the G.W. Fischer Building on Third

***Carl F. Gould**, Architect (1873-1939)*
Courtesy of Mrs. Anne Gould Hauberg
An artistically gifted architect with extensive archeological and historical knowledge.

***Olympic Hotel** (cat. 13)*
George B. Post & Sons, Architects
Bebb & Gould, Supervising Architects, c. 1923/1924
Courtesy of The NBBJ Group
Bebb & Gould were selected by Gould's former employer, the Manhattan firm of George B. Post & Sons, to administer the construction of the Olympic Hotel.

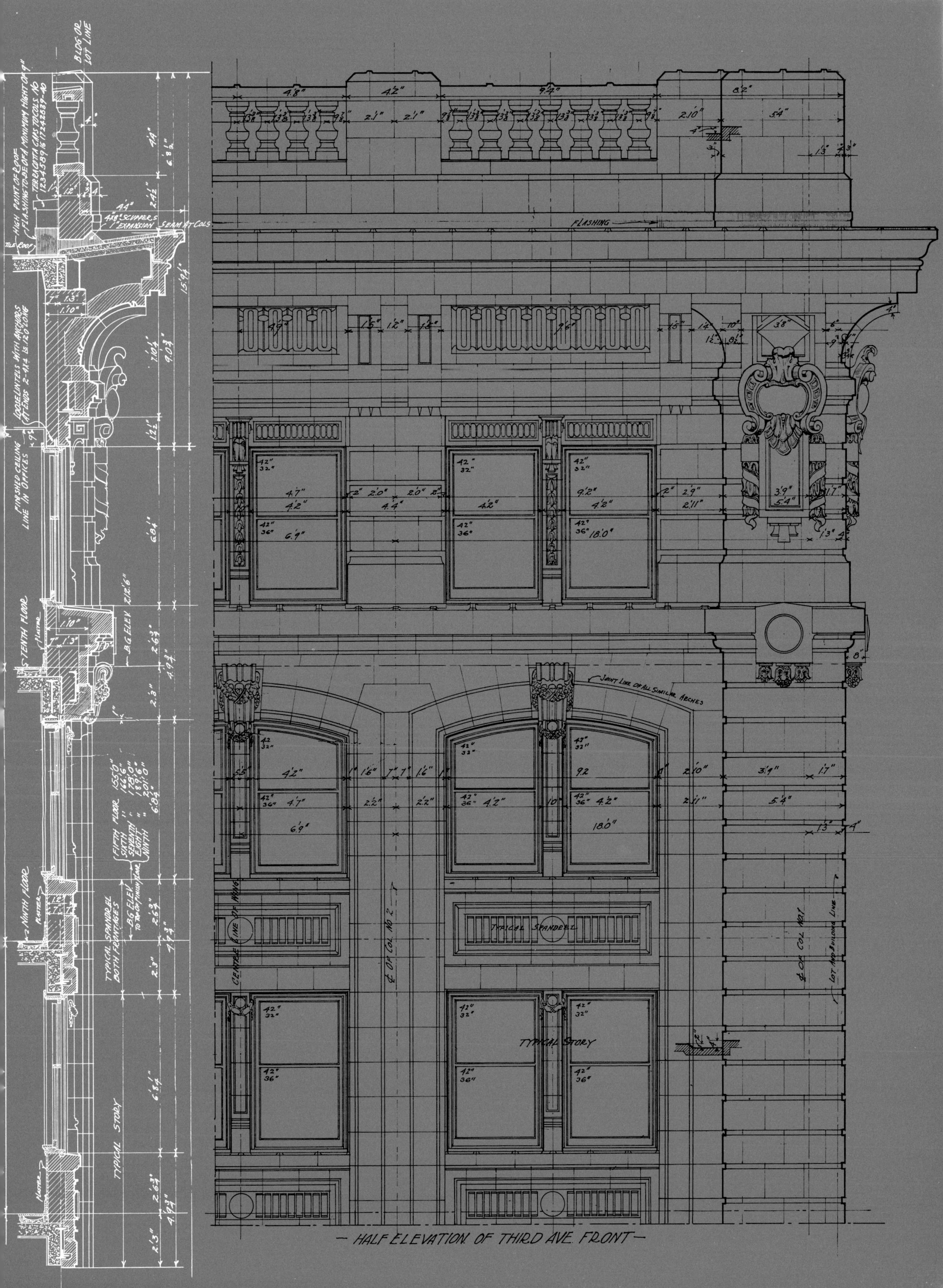

— HALF ELEVATION OF THIRD AVE. FRONT —

Fischer Studio Building *(cat. 72)*
Bebb & Mendell; Bebb & Gould, Architects
c. 1912/1915
Courtesy of Mrs. Anne Gould Hauberg
The seventh and eighth floors of the building housed a Ranaissance-revival style music hall flanked with two-story-high Corinthian columns.

Avenue. This project originated in the office of Bebb & Mendel in 1912. Planned as an eight-story steel structure, only three floors were constructed by 1914. Bebb and Gould redesigned the remaining five floors and modified the existing three floors to integrate the facade into a single, harmonious design. The seventh and eighth floors of the building interior housed a Renaissance revival style music hall flanked by two-story-high Corinthian columns. This space is expressed on the exterior of the building in a blank wall of terra-cotta ornamented with Venetian-inspired detail.

The Times Square Building of 1915 was the new firm's first architectural commission. It was designed for *The Seattle Times*, the city's leading newspaper at a time when five daily papers were published. The Blethen family, who own and publish *The Seattle Times* to this day, required a prestigious building to house their prominent paper. The site they selected for their new printing plant and publishing offices was a wedge-shaped lot bounded by Olive Street, Fourth Avenue and Fifth Avenue in the emerging commercial district. In 1915 this district was composed of two- and three-story wood-framed structures. The Times Square Building that arose on the site bore little relation to this humble context, purposely resembling more closely the Flatiron Building flanking Times Square in Manhattan. This new building was a "modern" structure with its fireproofed steel frame, reinforced concrete slab floors, and neo-classical terra-cotta-clad facade. This facade conformed to Gould's deeply instilled Beaux Arts principles, which are apparent in the design that perfectly proportions mass of wall to opening. Its banded floral relief provides perfect horizontal registration. Also to be noted are the deeply incised bedding joints, and the integration of architecture with sculpture. The major building entrance is signalled with a high-relief terra-cotta sculpture. It is allegorical and didactic, depicting the "muse" of telecommunication and the newspaper production process. This was the architecture of cosmopolitan corporate culture.

In October of 1915 construction commenced on Bebb and Gould's design for the offices of a news distributor, *The Puget Sound News*, now the Merchandise Mart on Second Avenue. This building was more modest in scale and ornamentation. It was a four-story concrete frame structure ornamented with terra-cotta in the English Gothic style. This style was well-suited to the narrow site as the large arched window openings allowed light to penetrate the deep space of the building.

In 1923 Bebb and Gould were selected by Gould's former employer, George B. Post & Sons, to administer the construction of the Olympic Hotel, a brick-clad structure ornamented with terra-cotta. Yet another major commission for the firm was the restrained, neo-classical tower for the Telephone Company in 1920. Bebb and Gould's final terra-cotta building was constructed in 1937 at 711 Second Avenue in the new Deco style. The firm's most extensive and accomplished assemblage of terra-cotta structures lies outside the commercial business district and the confines of this study in the original campus buildings for the University of Washington.

Bebb and Gould were to witness and participate in the metamorphosis of Seattle from a city of wood-framed storefronts to a city of terra-cotta-clad office towers. Their contributions to this new commercial district were refined structures that met or exceeded contemporary international architectural standards: an appropriate architecture for a city aspiring to be a world capital.

Times Square Building *(cat. 62)*
String Course Detail
Banded floral relief provides perfect horizontal registration.

Corona Hotel *(cat. 26)*
Bebb & Mendel, c. 1903
Second Avenue Storefront
Bebb's stylistic debt to Louis Sullivan is apparent in the horizontal facade organization and in the sinuous floral ornamentation of unglazed terra-cotta.

Times Square Building *(cat. 62)*
Bebb & Gould, Architects, c. 1915
Entry Typanum Sculpture
Allegorical and didactic terra-cotta sculpture depicting the "muse" of telecommunication and the newspaper production process.

6 The Architect of Tradition: John Graham, Sr.

Grant Hildebrandt

***John Graham Sr., Architect** (1873-1955)*

John Graham, Sr., practiced as an architect in Seattle from the turn of the century until the 1940s. He was prolific, designing many large and complex buildings. It would not be an exaggeration to say that he was a major shaper of the early twentieth-century face of Seattle. Fortunately, he was an architect of distinguished design skills.

Graham was a native of Liverpool. He received his architectural training through apprenticeship in England. This early training provided him with a sound sense for organization of an architectural plan and for accurate historical detail. It appears that he had no education in or inclination for architectural theory. Perhaps as a consequence, Graham had no dominant stylistic preference nor any developed personal idiom. His strengths were twofold: a skill in the appropriate and sensitive application of historic and modern architectural styles, and a fine eye for the proportion and nuance of ornament. Thus his buildings are recognizable and significant not because they signify an evolutionary or revolutionary architecture, but because of the often flawless artistry of their design within a variety of established modes.

Graham's most acclaimed buildings are the Exchange Building constructed in 1930 and the Ford Assembly Plant of 1913. However, neither of these structures qualifies for inclusion in this publication's inventory. The Exchange Building is made of cast stone and the Ford Assembly Plant, now the home of the Craftsman Press, lies outside the new boundaries of the downtown which define the focus area of this building survey. Fortunately, many of Graham's less publicized works do utilize terra-cotta and do stand in the heart of Seattle's commercial business district.

The Joshua Green Building of 1913, at 1425 Fourth Avenue, is a reinterpretation of the Chicago frame embellished with Baroque detail, the sort of thing that Daniel Burnham was doing in Chicago and elsewhere at the very close of the nineteenth century, or that Holabird and Roche were continuing to do well into the twentieth, as with their Brooks Building in Chicago of 1910. The Joshua Green Building, like the work of the great Chicagoans, keeps the ornament subordinate to the delicate frame with its great expanses of glass. Thus pilasters and string courses are delicate, attenuated; the false flat arches above the second floor, too thin to convey a real structural role, remind the viewer that this is, after all, only ornament, though ornament derived from an originally utilitarian role. Thus the ornament clads and enriches the light structural frame without overpowering it.

Unfortunately, numerous modifications to the original structure have not been kind. The orginal cornice has been removed and replaced with a crude sheet metal cap, the ground floor has been tastelessly remodeled, and the building name is now denoted with banal lettering. Today, one must observe the midsection of the building to comprehend its quality.

By contrast, The Savings Bank of Puget Sound building has recently undergone a sensitive restoration and is in mint condition. Originally built for the Bank of California in 1916, this building is notable for its use of a type of terra-cotta called "granitex." Granitex was terra-cotta glazed to resemble

***Dexter Horton Building** (cat. 24)*
Asahel Curtis photograph
Courtesy of the Washington State Historical Society
The arched entry north of the great columns is a tour-de-force of neo-Roman terra-cotta.

EXTER
ORTON
TIONAL
BANK
48046
THEL CURTIS

WASHINGT
BARTELL

granite. It was a popular, economical alternative to stone and is a thoroughly convincing imitation. Graham's design for this building is a superb example of the Greco-Roman style popular for banks in this era. It is rich with detail and perfect in proportion.

The Dexter Horton Building of 1922, at 710 Second Avenue, is perhaps Graham's finest terra-cotta-clad building. It is a large structure and Graham boldly grasped this massive scale. Immense gray granite attached columns fronting Second Avenue originally reflected the internal volume of the lobby and still convey the impression of a building with grand dimensions. With the exception of these columns, the building is almost entirely clad in sparkling, near-white, terra-cotta. Dentiled Greco-Roman cornices, scaled to the building's size, occur at three levels: above the windowed and cartouche-laden "entablature," capping the granite columns, and at the top and bottom of the uppermost two floors which form the building crown. The arched entry north of the great columns is a tour de force of Greco-Roman terra-cotta. In addition, the Dextor Horton Building is notable for its deep light wells located above the fourth floor on the south side of the building. Although by no means unique at this time, these light wells were a sensible and sculpturally powerful way to provide daylight to office spaces located within a large floor plan. Today the Dexter Horton Building's marvelous exterior of terra-cotta and granite remains largely unaltered and in use as offices for Seattle's city government.

Graham's terra-cotta building most familiar to the general public is the Frederick & Nelson department store of 1919. Unfortunately, it is far from being his best work. Admittedly, it lacks its original grand cornice. Nevertheless, the tan coloration of the terra-cotta is uninspired, the building mass is unrelieved by any variety or intensity

Medical-Dental Building *(cat. 55)*
Kreutzer & Albertson; John Graham, Sr., Architects, c. 1925
Venetian spandrels again at the fourteenth floor, a Venetian filigree of cusped ogee arches above, with blue inserts, then a series of setback penthouses and towers in filigree and blue.

Savings Bank of Puget Sound *(cat. 29)*
John Graham, Sr., Architect, c. 1908/1909
This building is notable for its use of "granitex," a type of terra-cotta glazed to resemble granite.

Nootka Investment Company *(cat. 45)*
John Graham, Sr., Architect, c. 1925
The columnar motif that frames the windows has Churrigueresque energy, but in fact has as its source the Jacobean Tower of Five Orders in the Bodleian Library at Oxford University.

of ornamentation, and its street level expression is modest when compared with Graham's design for another local department store, the Bon Marche with its inventive Art Deco marquees.

The Medical-Dental Building, originally Medical Arts, of 1925, at 505 Olive, is contiguous to and embraced by Frederick & Nelson, to which it provides an object lesson in delight. The first two floors have been badly rehashed; Venetian spandrels occur at the third floor; the fourth through thirteenth floors are rather plain—and then the fun starts. Venetian spandrels again at the fourteenth floor, a Venetian filigree of cusped ogee arches above, with blue inserts, then a series of setback penthouses and towers in filigree and blue. The best view of this skyline confectionery is from the north sidewalk on Stewart between Third and Fourth.

The Securities Building fronts the Stewart Street sidewalk. It is another of Graham's Greco-Roman designs executed in terra-cotta. The eastern half of this building, floors four through cornice, is a later addition and is identifiable by a change in the exterior coloration and detail. The ornament of the northern portion of the building along Third Avenue is especially fine, though it is now masked by a later marquee.

The Roosevelt Hotel of 1929, at Pine Street and Seventh Avenue, is an example of Graham's adoption of the Art Deco style late in his career. The ornament at the tops of the brick pilaster-like shafts and at the window spandrel panels is exemplary and is similar to that found on Graham's Exchange Building constructed in the same year. Unfortunately, the Roosevelt Hotel lacks sufficient ornament. What little ornament occurs is remote, located at upper levels of the building, and is of a restrained character. The unusual dearth of ornamentation and the date of construction for this building, which coincides with the year of the great stock market crash, engender the suspicion that budgetary constraints were significant.

One other terra-cotta structure designed by Graham remains to be mentioned. It is the tiny Nootka Investment Company at 715 Pike Street. Currently slated for demolition, this building sits abandoned, its ground floor hopelessly mutilated by storefront modifications. However, the second floor of this building remains unaltered and is a microcosm of delight. The columnar motif that frames the windows has Churrigueresque energy, but in fact has as its source the Jacobean Tower of Five Orders in the Bodleian Library at Oxford University. Graham has reinterpreted an ornamental example from his native country, and has done so with vitality. Though the scale is diminutive, this is as fine a piece of design as Graham ever produced, and that puts it in very good company indeed.

***Dexter Horton Building** (cat. 24)*
John Graham Sr., Architect, c. 1922
The Dexter Horton Building is perhaps Graham's finest terra-cotta-clad building. It is a large structure and Graham boldly grasped this massive scale.

***Frederick & Nelson Department Store** (cat. 59)*
John Graham, Sr., Architect, c. 1919
Asahel Curtis photograph
Courtesy of the Washington State Historical Society
The department store with its "original grand cornice."

HOTEL
Benjamin Franklin
VAUDEVILLE
ORPHEUM
The GREENE
MURDER CASE
WILLIAM POWELL
ALL TALKING
PARIS BOUND
55793
ASAHEL CURTIS

7 B. Marcus Priteca: Neoclassicism and the American Movie House

R. F. McCann

B. Marcus Priteca
(1889-1971)
Courtesy of R. F. McCann, Architect
An eclectic and experimental stylist, he was... predisposed to stone masonry.

Bethel Pentecostal Temple *(cat. 107)*
B. Marcus Priteca, Architect, c. 1915
The composition of terra-cotta facades proved in fact to be an opportunity for Priteca to indulge his love for shadow and ornamentation and to sculpt proportions on otherwise flat building surfaces.

One of the primary building types utilizing terra-cotta construction in the early twentieth century was the theater. Numerous and decoratively significant examples were built throughout Puget Sound. Most have long since fallen to redevelopment, but three of these single-purpose houses still remain: Seattle's Coliseum and Paramount Theaters and the Pantages in Tacoma. They were all designed by one of America's renowned theater architects, B. Marcus Priteca. An eclectic and experimental stylist, he was responsible for more than forty terra-cotta theaters throughout the United States.

Priteca's classical turn-of-the-century architectural education in Europe predisposed him to stone as the material of choice. Permanent and maintenance free, stone was the material of tradition. However, upon returning home, Priteca was confronted by the highly mechanized, accelerated construction processes underway in the America of the 1920s, as well as by the limited-term investment policies of American developers. Terra-cotta, not stone, matched their processes and their schedules. Thus nearly all the theater buildings he designed in a fifty-year career that began in 1910 were characterized by his use of terra-cotta and by his inclination for historic European styles.

Three-quarters of this theater work was commissioned by the Pantages theater, a chain located in the Western states and identified by its theaters' monochromatic white-to-beige palette, which is evident today on the Coliseum. Other terra-cotta projects include the polychromatic Natatorium and a pair of dark unglazed movie palaces: the Orpheum, which once stood on the Westin Hotel site, and the still extant Paramount.

Priteca's terra-cotta adaptations of classical architecture defined his personal design style. In the Coliseum he used terra-cotta to form a neo-classical cornice composition. Overhanging the building line, this cornice incorporated gutters, rain leaders and electrical lighting. Part of the interest this material held for Priteca was that it allowed him to design exteriors with customized molded units. The plasticity of it permitted him to appliqué the name of the theater in relief onto the face of the building. Similar techniques encouraged individual and creative surface treatments for the adjustment of proportions and a facade ornamentation that ranged from the Coliseum's Italian urns to French nymphs and Greek acanthus leaves. Moldings, spindles and spires characteristic of the Plateresque Period in Spanish architectural design are also to be found on his theaters.

Priteca's use of terra-cotta as a substitute for stone construction was undertaken with the knowledge of its special maintenance and moisture requirements. For this reason he provided specific instructions at the completion of each project in order that the owner could follow a maintenance program and undertake methods for cleaning to insure the longevity of the terra-cotta surface. The Coliseum in Seattle at Fifth and Pike has the only remaining cornice overhang of its style and size on the West Coast. Structural tests have indicated that this terra-cotta construction is stronger and far less susceptible to erosion than was the case with most other surviving cornices. Interim maintenance operations on the cornice in 1978 involved the removal of one tile unit and subsequent examination revealed that reinforcing steel bars and ties were used as redundant fastenings. Stonelike key slots between the inter-

Coliseum Theater *(cat. 60)*

B. Marcus Priteca, Architect, c. 1916

Priteca's terra-cotta adaptations of classical architecture defined his personal design style.

DATUM

locking units of the entablature added a further measure of security. Priteca's familiarity with stonework allowed him to place the cornice's center of gravity under the terra-cotta of the wall below.

Outset runs and the composition of terra-cotta facades proved in fact to be an opportunity for Priteca to indulge his love for shadow and ornamentation and to sculpt proportions on otherwise flat building surfaces. Sciography is the study of sun angles to determine the extent of overhang and outset which each horizontal band and stone course requires to achieve classical architectural proportions. Knowledge of it was required in the European academies where Priteca was trained. His education promulgated solutions to all kinds of practical problems, such as the incorporation of drip edges onto rain sills and moldings. This was an especially important consideration with the light monochromatic exteriors he frequently employed so as to prevent rain streaking and staining of these pale vertical surfaces.

The Northwest's wet climate dictated the use of highly glazed terra-cotta as opposed to the more porous unglazed units found in California. This prevented moisture penetration to the interior cells of the units. Happily, this use of glazed terra-cotta in Seattle and Tacoma has bequeathed to us uniquely designed theaters that remain in relatively good repair. In fact, one such structure, though partially collapsed due to the deterioration of the wood roof, still remains in otherwise good condition thanks to the terra-cotta exterior. Similarly, the original terra-cotta front of the Capitol Theater in Yakima, Washington, designed by an associate of Priteca's, survived a fire and a complete reconstruction of its interior.

The terra-cotta industry, perhaps more than any other, appreciated Priteca's understanding and advancement of the material. Molds of Priteca's details became catalogue items. Almost anywhere that classical ornamental styles of terra-cotta remain on the West Coast, the specific elements and ornamental motifs of Priteca's original detailing can be found.

Ornament in the Gladding-McBean Collection
Courtesy of R. F. McCann, Priteca's file
Much of the ornamental and flat ashlar or veneer pieces were standard forms that the manufacturers kept in stock or could produce quickly and easily.

Coliseum Theater
(cat. 60)
Elevation of the Pike St. Facade
Courtesy of R. F. McCann, Architect
One of the primary building types that terra-cotta construction of the early twentieth century addressed was theaters. Numerous and decoratively significant examples peppered the Puget Sound urban landscape.

Coliseum Theater
(cat. 60)
Construction
J.D. Cress Photograph
Courtesy of Bittman, Vammen, Taylor PS
Returning home, however, Priteca was confronted by the highly mechanized, accelerated construction processes underway in the 1920s...

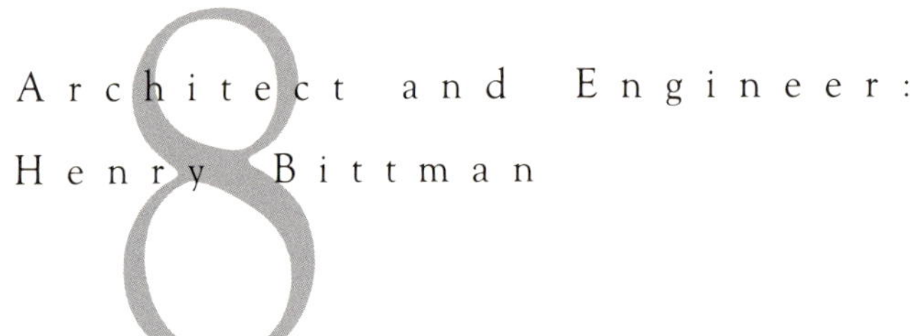

Architect and Engineer: Henry Bittman

Karin Link

Terminal Sales Building Entry *(cat. 110)*
Henry Bittman, Architect, c. 1923
The wide window bays provide this large building with a feeling of openness and light. The light-colored and shiny terra-cotta cladding that goes up to the second floor of the facade accentuates this impression, giving the building a sense of human scale.

The office of Henry Bittman enjoyed great success and renown during Seattle's building boom of the 1920s. This success was the result of Bittman's abilities as a structural engineer and his working relationship with Harold Adams, an architect, who is rarely mentioned in the history of Northwest architecture. Bittman's office's most impressive work can still be seen today in downtown Seattle, heavily adorned, if not clad, in terra-cotta.

The education of American engineers, and especially architects practicing in the 1920s, varied greatly. John Roebling, the engineer of the Brooklyn Bridge, had pursued what was essentially an architectural education. Frank Lloyd Wright pursued engineering studies, but became an architect. In general, the division between the fields of architecture and engineering was not as marked as it is today. Bittman studied engineering and practiced as a structural engineer. He also became a licensed architect and the head of a distinguished architectural engineering firm. Today it is ironic to learn that although his firm received commissions for many important projects, such as the addition to the King County Courthouse, several of Bittman's contemporaries, including B. Marcus Priteca, resented his involvement in architecture. They felt he had come to architecture "through the back door" as it were; he was even nicknamed "three-band Bittman." True, several of his buildings displayed such common characteristics as a tripartite organization of either all or part of a facade, wide spanning door or ground floor openings surmounted by a dropped arch, and strong vertical elements articulating facades. But Bittman's designs were often complex and the criticisms leveled by his contemporaries now seem, at best, simplistic. His mastery of architectural form came from his association with architects such as Harold Adams, who had a hand in most of the office's work. Bittman's and Adams' professional relationship must have been similar to that of Adler and Sullivan, engineer and architect respectively, a common relationship in the late nineteenth and early twentieth centuries.

Raison d'Etre Cafe
Terminal Sales Building
The interior of the building has been remodeled in many places; but the lobby and the old clubroom (presently the "Raison d'Etre Cafe") on the mezzanine floor give a clear sense of the original design with its inviting and interesting spaces.

Terminal Sales Building *(cat. 110)*
Henry Bittman, Architect, c. 1923
The Terminal Sales Building is an excellent example of the successful integration of structure with architectural elements. When it was built in 1923, it was the tallest flat slab structure west of the Mississippi.

SAMPLE

Since the demarcation between the disciplines of architecture and engineering was less clear than today, greater cooperation between architect and engineer was possible. As a result, structural and architectural form were carefully integrated. Bittman's office produced a wide range of buildings differing widely in style and form. They show not only his mastery of very different architectural styles (the Eagles Auditorium Building and the Olympic Tower, for example), but also Bittman's skill as a structural engineer.

The Terminal Sales Building is an excellent example of the successful integration of structure with architectural elements. When it was built in 1923, it was the tallest flat slab structure west of the Mississippi. Bittman was clearly an innovative structural engineer in his day. He knew how to create more open space, wider spans and taller buildings. The Terminal Sales Building is also remarkable in terms of design. The Neo-Gothic ornament of its rosettes and its shields and bands of fruit meshes harmoniously with the basic structure of the building and with the brick and polished granite of the facade. The wide window bays provide this large building with a feeling of openness and light. The light-colored and shiny terra-cotta cladding that goes up to the second floor of the facade accentuates this impression, giving the building a sense of human scale. There is a clear awareness of structure, scale, ornament and the interplay of the color and texture of differing materials.

The interior of the building has been remodeled in many places; but the lobby and the old clubroom (presently the Raison d'Etre Cafe) on the mezzanine floor still give a clear sense of the original design with its inviting and interesting spaces. Although the lobby has been remodeled somewhat since 1923, judging by contemporary promotional literature its best features remain. The Gothic ornament is in keeping with the building's exterior and this interior space is articulated both by a major arch at its center, creating two large areas, as well as a series of widely spaced door and window openings. This lobby is divided into two levels and its design gives a sense of spaciousness, height, and uniqueness.

At the mezzanine level, one of a series of large clubrooms, originally designed for the merchants to whom the building was dedicated, is divided in half by woodworking on the ceilings that delineates two polygonal shapes. These ceiling shapes are picked up in the capitals of the large, encrusted, octagonal piers at the two corners of the room and at the convergence of these two ceiling polygons. As with the lobby, what could have been an unimpressive space has been given a sense of greater scale and visual interest. A similar appreciation of spatial effects can be seen at the entry to the Eagles Auditorium Building.

Bittman's office also produced several small-scale buildings that show a strong sense of design. The Decatur Building, for example, has a very human scale. What is especially remarkable about this building is the meshing of the purely classical ornament with the "modern" skin of terracotta, which at a quick glance is similar in color to the stone of certain ancient Greek temples. This is a simple, unpretentious building, yet with its delicate use of classical ornament and with its golden color it is reminiscent of Classical Greek bas-reliefs, achieving real elegance.

Who were the designers of these buildings? Harold Adams was well known in his day as a designer and draughtsman and in great demand by the major Seattle architectural offices. Adams was born in 1885 in Danville, Illinois. His father operated a brick-selling business and later a porcelain and china shop. Adams studied architecture at the University of Illinois at Champaign. He arrived in Seattle around 1908 and probably joined the Bittman office soon after. During the next twenty years he moved around between the offices of Bittman, John Graham Sr., Bebb & Gould and several other major architectural firms. While employed by John Graham Sr., he had an important role in the design of the Frederick & Nelson department store.

Adams' abilities as a draughtsman can be seen in his drawings of the Olympic Tower and the Eagles Auditorium. In later years he was a friend and pupil of Mark Tobey. Something of a bohemian, he liked boats and collected bric-à-brac from the shops on

Downtown Mini-Warehouse *(cat. 97)*
Henry Bittman, Architect, c. 1928
Photographer Unknown
Courtesy of Bittman, Vammen, Taylor PS
They were especially proficient at selecting the appropriate glaze for each design and letting the natural shiny quality of Northwest terra-cotta enhance the appearance of these buildings.

First Avenue. He had a fine collection of cloisonné, underlining his personal interest in ornamentation. Like many architects at that time, he traveled to Europe and apparently developed a fondness for Gothic architecture. This affection may explain why many of his designs bear an affinity to the English Gothic style in their vertical elements. Adams was clearly appreciative of the architectural styles of Classicism, Neo-Classicism and Beaux Arts design, as can be seen in the formal spaces and ornament of the Eagles Building, the old clubroom of the Terminal Sales Building, or in the purer classicism of the Decatur Building. Despite his talents, Adams was a quiet and unassuming man.

Bittman, on the other hand, appears to have been a somewhat flamboyant and amusing character. He was a dapper dresser, wearing a winged collar and bow tie. In his later years he was proud of his bald forehead and his ruff of long white curls at the back of his head. Born in New York City in 1881, he was the son of a prominent New York interior designer, who was retained by such illustrious clients as

Henry Bittman
(1881-1953)
Bittman, the engineer, raised in an artistic environment, displayed an almost stereotypical artistic temperament.

Henry Bittman (center right) Henry Adams (center left) and staff
Photographer Unknown
Courtesy of Bittman, Vammen, Taylor PS
Bittman's and Adams' professional relationship must have been similar to that of Adler and Sullivan, engineer and architect respectively...

***Decatur Building** (cat. 57)*
Henry Bittman, Architect, c. 1921
Bittman's office also produced several small-scale buildings that show a strong sense of design. The Decatur Building, for example... is a simple, unpretentious building, yet with its delicate use of classical ornament and with its golden color it is reminiscent of Classical Greek bas-reliefs, achieving real elegance.

***Securities Building** (cat. 96)*
John Graham Sr. and Frank Allen, Architects, c. 1912/1915
Frequently, Bittman could be seen walking through the streets of Seattle, a very noticeable figure with his winged collar and bow tie rounding up friends and acquaintances who later took office space in the Securities Building.

J.P. Morgan. He studied at Cooper Union and the Pratt Institute in New York and may have pursued further study at the Armour Institute in Chicago. His education focused primarily on structural engineering. When he first came to Seattle in 1906, he was a bridge designer. Later that year he formed a partnership with the architect William Kingsley, but this dissolved by 1907. By 1910 he had opened Bittman Architects/Engineers. During his early years in the Seattle area, he lived a bohemian existence in Newcastle, Washington, where he and his wife, Jessie, entertained increasingly annoying hangers-on. Tired of the artistic lifestyle, Bittman and his wife, a famous horticulturist, moved to the Wallingford neighborhood of Seattle. Bittman remained socially active and joined many of the major clubs in Seattle. He went frequently to the theater and opera. His involvement in theatrics no doubt explains why his office designed several important theaters, including the Eagles Auditorium and the Music Box.

Bittman was an astute businessman as well as a good structural engineer. His notebooks show carefully itemized costs for each building, complete with a quick, small sketch of a floorplan and a section, as well as basic notes on structure, all on one 8½" x 11" sheet. One anecdote in particular reveals his gregariousness and his talents as an entrepreneur: he had an arrangement with the owners of the Securities Building where his office was located that if he could solicit tenants for the year, he would receive a month's rent free. Frequently, Bittman could be seen walking through the streets of Seattle, a very noticeable figure, rounding up friends and acquaintances, who later took office space in the Securities Building. He always got his rent free.

Following World War II terra-cotta became prohibitively expensive; at the same time the ideology of the Modern design movement rejected the application of historicist ornaments. Bittman's office could no longer produce elegant terra-cotta buildings. Later the office produced improved and fireproofed housing on First Hill and made many contributions to structural steel design. Bittman participated in the design of the P.I. Building and served on the committee that selected the P.I. Globe, the neon advertisement that still illuminates our skyline. Adams continued to work at Bittman's office until Bittman's death in 1953. At this time, the office was taken over by his nephew, Herbert Bittman, and an associate, Dean Sanders, who had been employed by Henry Bittman since 1945. This office is still in existence in Seattle.

The most notable products of Henry Bittman's office were the terra-cotta clad and decorated buildings of the 1920s, especially those displaying Adams' talents. These men were two very different personalities yet they formed a powerful design collaborative. Adams, the architect, quiet and unpretentious, possessed the artistic and architectural sense that ensured the office's success. Bittman, the engineer, raised in an artistic environment, displayed an almost stereotypical artistic temperament. Yet he also possessed an understanding of building structure and an excellent business sense. The two men complemented one another both in knowledge and temperament. At the same time terra-cotta was a material admirably suited to their designs. They were especially proficient at selecting the appropriate glaze for each design and letting the natural shiny quality of Northwest terra-cotta enhance the appearance of these buildings. These well-designed and irreplaceable buildings have a special place in the history of Northwest architecture. The exact combination of talents, clients and exuberance that spawned the Bittman and Adams buildings can never again occur. But the people of Seattle are fortunate that it did happen here and that many of the products of that union remain to enrich their city.

***Olympic Tower** (cat. 71)*
Henry Bittman, Architect, c. 1929
The exact combination of talents, clients and exuberance that spawned the Bittman buildings can never again occur. But the people of Seattle are fortunate that it did happen here and that many of the products of that union remain to enrich their city.

the FRANKFURTER

9 Art Deco and Terra-Cotta: F.W. Woolworth Building

Ellen Miller-Wolfe

Design for an Office Tower (unbuilt)
Victor N. Jones & Associates, c. 1935
Courtesy of Jones & Jones
Modernistic facades incorporated the strenuous vertical elements and decorative embellishment most often found at entries, staggered rooflines, and recessed spandrels...

The Art Deco or Modernistic style was popularized for American audiences at the 1925 Exposition des Arts Decoratifs in Paris. The style broke with the staid Beaux Arts tradition which had characterized architecture for decades. Modernistic facades incorporated the strenuous vertical elements and decorative embellishment most often found at entries, staggered rooflines, and recessed spandrels. The ornamental vocabulary of Art Deco included spiral, reed, vine and floral ornament, often borrowed from Art Nouveau and Mayan traditions, as well as geometric and streamlined embellishment gleaned from the new cubist paintings and automobile designs.

Terra-cotta, with its plasticity, variety of textures and finishes, durability and color range was a perfect medium for the smooth surfaces, stamped and lattice-like ornament, and polychrome treatments that often characterized Art Deco architecture.

In Seattle there are very few examples of terra-cotta buildings with Art Deco styling. The city's most exuberant Art Deco expressions are found on the interiors of buildings, in particular the Seattle Art Museum, the Exchange Building and the Seattle Tower. The latter two buildings have entrance lobbies with dazzling gold Art Deco ornament set against dark, polished stone, reminiscent of the flamboyant movie palaces of the 1920s. Cast stone and masonry materials are used on the exteriors of these and other Art Deco examples more often than terra-cotta, with two notable exceptions: the Olympic Tower and the Woolworth Building, located in the downtown retail core.

Consider first the Exchange Building, a Modernistic skyscraper faced in ochre-colored cast stone. The architect, John Graham, used the geometric and spiral ornament of Art Deco, together with original agricultural symbols, which reinforced the use of the building as a Merchant's Exchange. The Hartford Building, bordering Pioneer Square, features a severe cast stone facade, trimmed with Art Deco ornament at the pier caps. The Seattle Tower, an early Modernistic landmark, features a brick veneer facade embellished with brown-colored terra-cotta. Whereas the color of the terra-cotta blends with the brick, its intricate texturing and details highlight recessed spandrels and a staggered roofline, contrasting with the regularity of brick coursing and the unbroken, vertical thrust of the piers.

The Olympic Tower and the Woolworth Building border Third Avenue in Seattle's retail core. Both buildings incorporate Modernistic elements and are fully clad in terra-cotta. The Olympic Tower possesses verticality, setbacks and Mayan ornament, all Modernnistic features, while its truncated roof and Moorish-style balconies have the eclectic feel of an earlier time.

The F.W. Woolworth Company Building (1940) is a late and simplified expression of the Art Deco that also reflects the streamlined Moderne style that succeeded it. Angled wings that culminate in a truncated corner tower express, in miniature, the familiar Modernistic profile. The vertical thrust of earlier Modernism, fully realized in the Seattle Tower and Olympic Tower, is tempered here. Wide, cream-colored, fluted terra-cotta piers that alternate with darker, salmon-colored, recessed spandrels, lend a rippled or corrugated effect that is enunciated in the staggered roofline. Vine and floral terra-cotta ornament is subordinated to the vertical bands that encapsulate it,

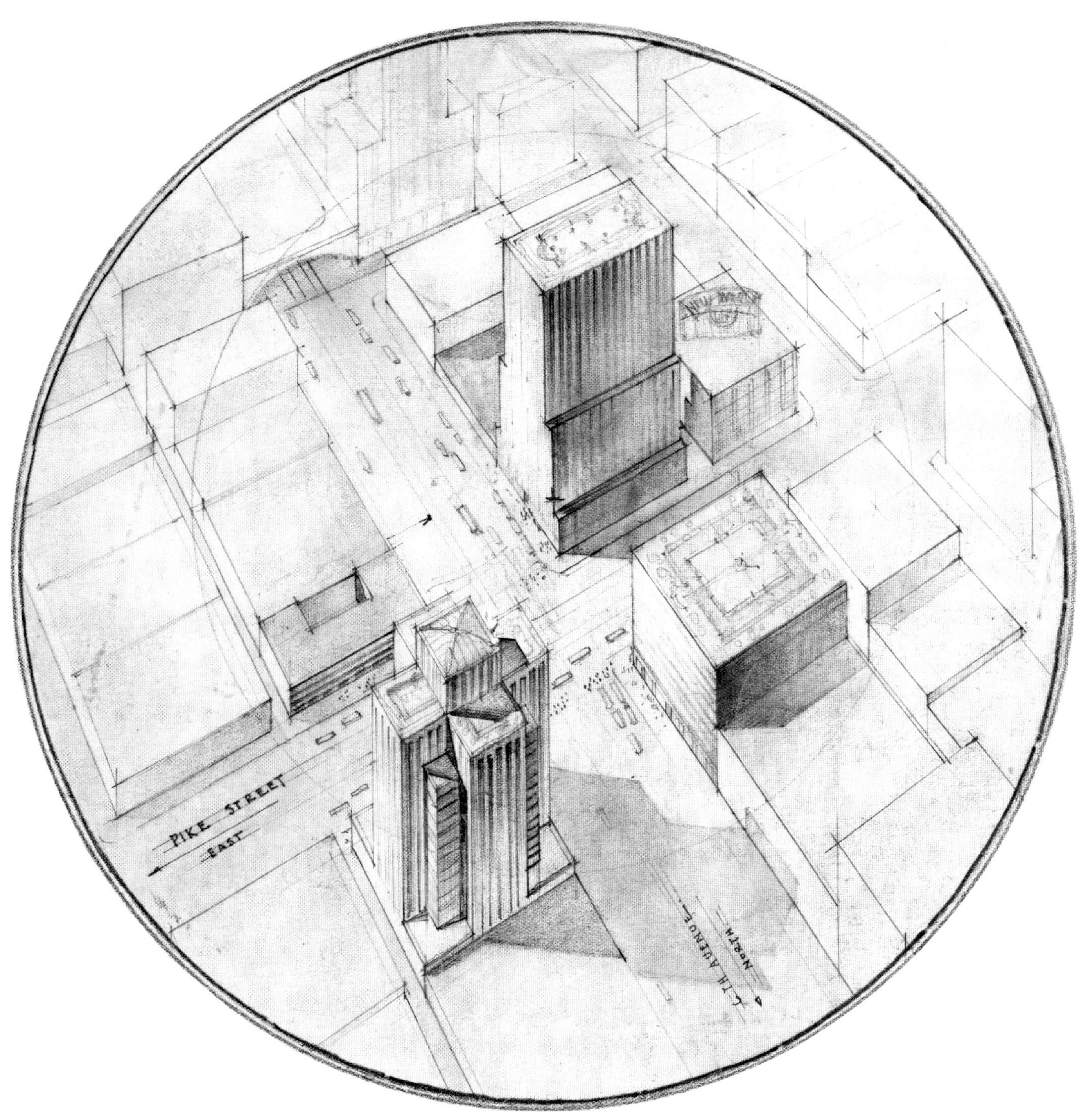

Proposed Development for Sixth Avenue and Pine Street

Victor N. Jones & Associates, c. 1935
Courtesy of Jones & Jones
Unbuilt Art Deco skyscrapers would have sculptured Seattle's skyline with their staggered rooflines.

Deco Moderne Styling
Victor N. Jones & Associates, c. 1935
Courtesy of Jones & Jones
...the city's most exuberant Art Deco expressions are found on the interiors of buildings...

characteristic of Art Deco.

Functional simplicity overtakes finicky ornament at the broad, flat salmon-colored band that separates retail from storage uses and carries the familiar gold lettering announcing the company name, surmounted by a narrow frieze of running chevrons.

The effect of this border is to direct eyes downward and thus shoppers toward merchandise. Originally, the retail front was permeated by several entries that alternated with cube-like storefront bays—references to earlier, smaller commercial blocks and more personalized shopping. In recent years, entries have been removed to better control traffic in and out of the building. Display windows, their joints downplayed, now give a light, streamlined look to the retail frontage. The principal corner entry features Moderne styling in the form of streamlined metal door surrounds. Above the corner entry, a Deco-inspired gold clock with flanking band wings alludes to civic clock towers, albeit upside down, of a bygone era.

Apart from its Art Deco styling and terra-cotta composition, Woolworth's is of interest as a forerunner of stereotypical, three-dimensional, billboard architecture, scrutinized by Robert Venturi and Denise Scott Brown in their book, *Learning from Las Vegas.* Building design is focused on conveying the image and product of a particular business in this genre of architecture. For easy recognition and immediate association, the Woolworth Company simplified the design elements of the Art Deco, much as an artist renders a cartoon character with a few, deft strokes of his pen.

Cream and salmon terra-cotta and gold lettering were repeated across the country, conveying the reliability and reach of this giant company. Moreover, by using the Art Deco style that had, by 1940, become conventional, Woolworth's directed its appeal to popular tastes. For it was the masses, not the avant garde, who were the mainstay of this five-and-ten-cent store.

Coincidentally, this particular building is somewhat like a billboard; the facade was applied in part to a preexisting commercial structure that stood on Third Avenue.

To characterize the F.W. Woolworth Company Building as a stereotype, is, in some people's minds, to belittle it. However, when one compares it to its roadside successors and other downtown buildings, its merits are obvious. In the ways that it compares to other stereotypical buildings, it stands in fanciful and lively contrast to the many anonymous office structures located downtown. Unlike its roadside counterparts, of which it has been said "There is no there there," the configuration of Woolworth's both embraces and defines its street corner, providing light and air to what is fast becoming a crowded corridor of downtown. Its correspondence to other downtown Modernistic and terra-cotta buildings lends it a sense of place and theme that overrides its ubiquity.

In closing, it is worth noting the revival of many of the characteristics of the Woolworth Building. A recent *New York Times* article entitled "The Grand Reach of Corporate Architecture" (January 20, 1985), observed that businesses were again asking their designers to "cast company logos across America's skyline." In doing so, architects are turning back to the sculpted towers, polychrome facades and Art Deco styling of the earlier twentieth century. All the more reason to take another look at our fine stock of Art Deco, terra-cotta buildings and examine their unique contribution to the Seattle cityscape.

Vance Building (cat. 70)
V.W. Voorhees; John Graham, Sr., Architects, c. 1929
Spiral, reed, vine and floral ornament, often borrowed from Art Nouveau and Mayan traditions...

Woolworth's Store (cat. 69)
Harold B. Hamhill, Architect, 1939
The configuration of Woolworth's both embraces and defines its street corner, providing light and air to what is fast becoming a crowded corner of downtown.

JOSEPH VANCE
BUILDING
WOOLWORTH'S

10 Terra-Cotta, the Urban Streetscape and the Need for Diversity

Victor Gardaya

1929 Streetscape
Asahel Curtis Photograph
Courtesy of the Washington State Historical Society
City districts... need to function as combinations of manufacturing, commercial, residential and entertainment zones...

Terra-cotta. Literally, "cooked earth." Chemically a compound of silica, alumina and metal oxides. Technologically, a cast and fired mixture of shale and clays which are often glazed. Historically, not unrelated to the colored faiences of the Mesopotamian city states of Ur and Kish or the west Asian empires of Babylon and Persia. Categorically, falling into the one-tenth of building construction that concerns itself with aesthetics, that fraction most vulnerable to economics, that part frequently termed architecture. An ancient process. A ubiquitous material, delicate in appearance, plastic in its manufacture, brittle in its application, impervious to time and the weather, ineffable in its effect.

From the street, terra-cotta is the glint of specular light off the knife edge of a surface; the wash of brightness and shadow over a cornice; the glazed cladding half obscured by graffiti; the seemingly chiseled relief above a doorway; the shock of color in a medallion. If the classic definition of architecture is "commodity, firmness and delight," then terra-cotta's emphasis—preponderantly and without apology—is on the delightful and diverse human usage to which architecture is put.

Twenty-four years ago in *The Death and Life of Great American Cities* Jane Jacobs described the indispensable components of urban diversity. By now they are an urban planning cliché, nevertheless they bear repeating. City districts must serve more than one primary purpose. There is first the need to function as combinations of manufacturing, commercial, residential and entertainment zones in order to ensure that people will use these districts at all hours of the day and evening. Second, neighborhoods must contain a mix of buildings that vary in scale, age, and condition in order to promote opportunities for the largest array of would-be residents and fledgling entrepreneurs. Third, and as a natural consequence of the first two premises, there has to be a vigorous concentration of people who work, shop and dwell in such districts.

Seattle's terra-cotta buildings make an unparalleled contribution to our urban diversity as historic artifacts; as variegated and human-scaled building stock; as decorated and expressionist architecture; as stage sets for the street theater which is our commercial life; and, in Walter Benjamin's endearing phrase, "...as commodities, objects of speculation, and instruments of ideology."

As historic entities, Seattle's terra-cotta dates from the Great Fire to the Alaskan Gold Rush, from the fin-de-siècle and the Alaska-Yukon Pacific Exposition to World War I, from the onset of the Jazz Age to the middle of the Depression. Stylistically, these buildings range from reticent Greek to vaguely Italianate, from Romanesque and Gothic to German Renaissance, from Spanish Moor to Venetian and Florentine, from P.T. Barnum to Morris Lapidus and back again. This vivid eclecticism, this carnival showmanship, this Walt Disney approach to the business of architecture was considered eminently defensible by contemporaneous historians of the built

***Alexis Hotel** (cat. 37)*
Max Umbrecht, Architect, c. 1901
View Up Madison
Asahel Curtis Photograph
Courtesy of the Washington State Historical Society
Terra-cotta buildings... as historic artifacts, as variegated and human scaled building stock, as decorated and expressionist architecture, as stage sets for the street theater which is our commercial life...

IT'S
Rainier
BEER
THERE'S NEW VIGOR & STRENGTH IN EVERY DROP
THE
HOFBRAU
CAFE
COMA
APOLIS FLYER
50¢
ROUND TRIP
SIGNS
THE MADISON
RESTAURANT
YMCA
3489

Sailors Union of the Pacific *(cat. 113)*

Ultimately, time has positioned these buildings "... even the most amateurish, at the level of art!"

York Lunch *(cat. 80)*

J. Lister Holmes, Architect, c. 1924

Utterly human scaled themselves, they have an ameliorating effect on the towers that have come to surround them.... This telescoping effect, this incredibly cinematic device, allows us to comprehend that which is incomprehensible.

environment. Alois Riegle in 1893 described the need for decoration as "...one of the most elementary needs of man; indeed more elementary than the need to protect his body." Paul Frankl in 1914 wrote that "...architecture is the moulded theater of human activity."

Admittedly, these are revisionists speaking in opposition to Hegel's historical determinist, Pugin's religious and Viollet-le-Duc's rationalist interpretations of architecture. Admittedly also, these debates raged within the European academies well removed from the hurly-burly of Seattle's streets. Nonetheless, the newer permissiveness granted local architects the license, if such were required, to create a fanciful world full of Gothic business colleges and Moorish swimming pools. And what of these buildings today with their compromised stylistic legitimacy?

Paraphrasing Susan Sontag's tract *On Photography* "...they are only fragments and with the passage of time their moorings have become unstuck. They have drifted into a soft abstract pastness, open to any kind of reading." In fact, they are memento mori. Ultimately, time has positioned these buildings "...even the most amateurish, at the level of art."

As products of their time, Seattle's terra-cotta buildings bestow a further diversifying legacy. The scale of these structures at two, five, seven and twelve stories contributes a necessary syncopation, a disarming shift of accents to the city's composition. Utterly human in scale themselves, they have an ameliorating effect on the towers that have come to surround them. In other words, the picturesqueness of a terra-cotta door or window surround humanizes the five-storied edifice as a whole, and it, in turn, tames the fifty-storied late modernist tower. This telescoping effect, this cinematic device allows us to comprehend that which is incomprehensible. To brush one's fingers against the indented and convex terra-cotta detailing while

Mann Building *(cat. 75)*

Henry Bittman and Sherwood Ford, Architects, c. 1926

From the stained glass in the First United Methodist to the stained oeuvre of the Embassy Theater and all the hoary honky tonks in between...

EMBASSY
CATHOUSE FEVER
ALSO
DIXIE RAY
EMBASSY
CATHOUSE FEV
DIXIE RAY
HE TURF
Grill
CIGARS
1407
THE TURF
Hottest Show In Town!
1409
EXIT
THE BEST IN ADULT Entertainment
FOR MATURE ADULTS 18 and OVER
FOR MATURE ADULTS 18 and OVER

strolling past as children do, to sense the rhythms and textures of the middle stories, to visually climb the setbacks and ziggurat forms of the pinnacles of these buildings, is to know innately that they are scaled to your own physical dimensions, your width, your height. Playful embodiments of the pathetic fallacy, anthropomorphic as no modernist architecture could be, they are the closest thing we possess to the Renaissance depictions of the idealized man-built environment.

Giotto's *The Meeting of Joachim and Anna* might have occurred in the front portal of a dozen buildings downtown. Lorenzetti's *Peaceful City* might have been painted from the Alaskan Way Viaduct. Ghiberti's *Gates of Paradise* might have been modeled from a thousand local studio windows. Masaccio's *The Holy Trinity* and Alberti's translation of it from pigment into stone at Mantua is the great coffered barrel vault of the Dexter Horton Building. Veronese's *Christ in the House of Levi* is the front portico of the St. Charles Hotel. Ghirlandaio, Perugino, Mantegna and Raphael have all been blatantly, shamelessly replicated here in ways no better or worse than postcard misrepresentations from the Louvre. These imitations in terra-cotta of details from the Italian masters are Seattle's first grappling with "aesthetic consumerism," our first faltering step toward the city as a work of art. To quote Aldo Rossi: "How are collective urban artifacts related to works of art? All great manifestations of social life have in common with the work of art the fact that they are born in unconscious life. This life is collective in the former, individual in the latter; but this is only a secondary difference because one is a product of the public and the other is for the public: the public provides the common denominator."

"People are part of architecture" Frankl wrote. Nowhere is this more clearly illustrated than in the accommodation of the sacred and the profane. From the stained glass in the United First Methodist Church to the stained oeuvre of the Embassy Theater, and all the hoary honky-tonks in between, what other building material or architectural style is as hospitable to the neon razzmatazz, the hand-scrawled signage, the whole *Learning From Las Vegas*/Venturiesque iconography of the late twentieth-century American streetscape? What other architecture could hold its own against

Decatur Building
(cat. 57)
Henry Bittman, Architect, c. 1921
Elevation of the Sixth Avenue Facade
Courtesy of Bittman, Vammen, Taylor PS
Categorically, falling into that one-tenth of building construction which concerns itself with aesthetics, that fraction most vulnerable to economics, that part frequently termed architecture.

Decatur Building
(cat. 57)
Photographer unknown
Courtesy of Bittman, Vammen, Taylor PS
Paraphrasing Susan Sontag, these buildings "...are only fragments and with the passage of time their moorings have become unstuck. They have drifted into a soft abstract pastness, open to any kind of reading."

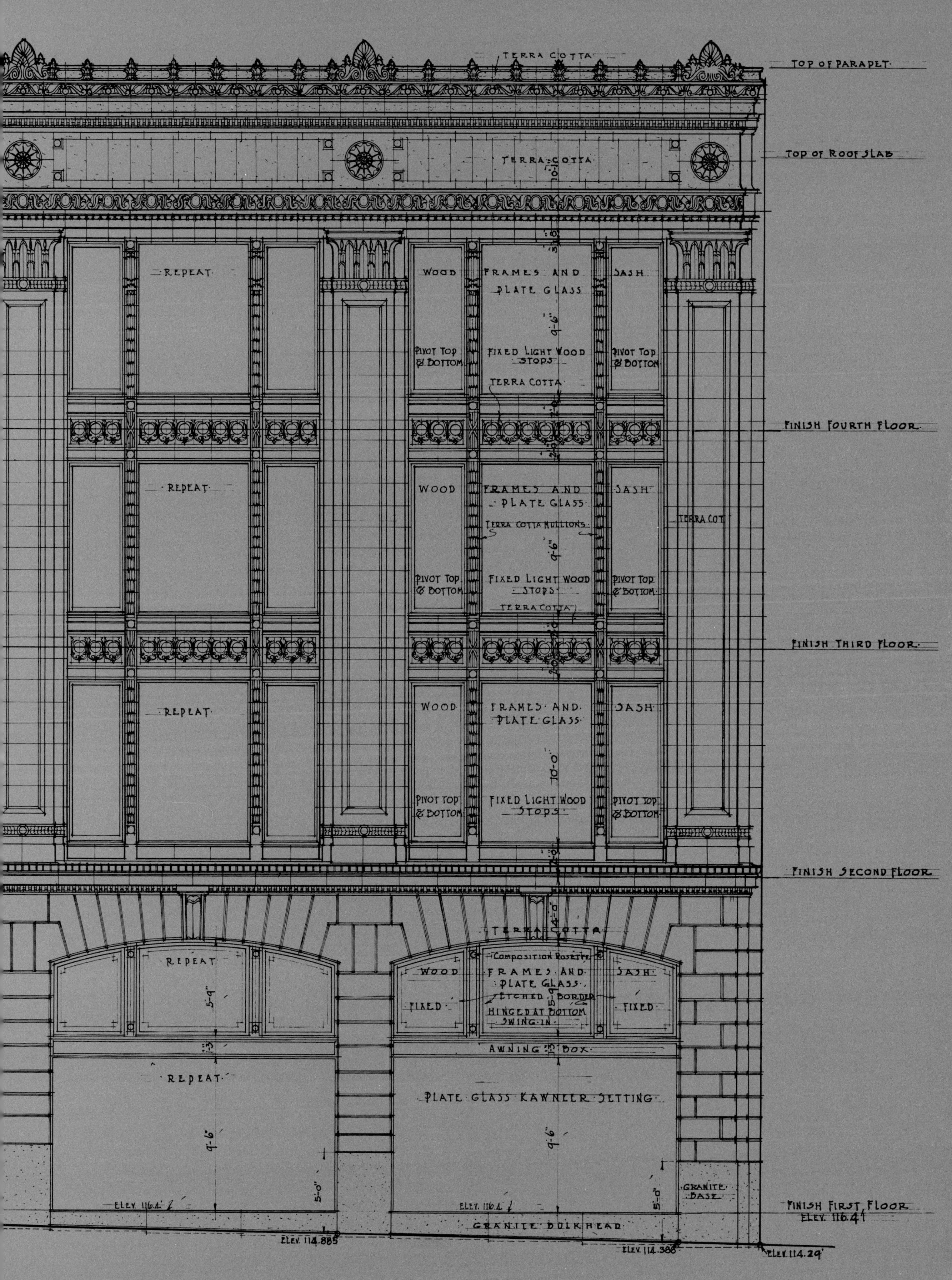
TERRA COTTA
TOP OF PARAPET
TERRA COTTA
TOP OF ROOF SLAB
REPEAT
WOOD FRAMES AND SASH
PLATE GLASS
PIVOT TOP & BOTTOM
FIXED LIGHT WOOD STOPS
TERRA COTTA
FINISH FOURTH FLOOR
REPEAT
WOOD FRAMES AND SASH
PLATE GLASS
TERRA COTTA MULLIONS
TERRA COT
PIVOT TOP & BOTTOM
FIXED LIGHT WOOD STOPS
TERRA COTTA
FINISH THIRD FLOOR
REPEAT
WOOD FRAMES AND SASH
PLATE GLASS
PIVOT TOP & BOTTOM
FIXED LIGHT WOOD STOPS
FINISH SECOND FLOOR
TERRA COTTA
REPEAT
COMPOSITION ROSETTE
WOOD FRAMES AND SASH
PLATE GLASS
ETCHED BORDER
FIXED
HINGED AT BOTTOM SWING IN
AWNING BOX
REPEAT
PLATE GLASS KAWNEER SETTING
GRANITE BASE
ELEV. 116.4
FINISH FIRST FLOOR ELEV. 116.41
GRANITE BULKHEAD
ELEV. 114.885
ELEV. 114.388
ELEV. 114.29

the indignity and exuberance of our commercial life in this zone where architectural ego clashes against vernacular necessity? Certainly not the Modern Movement's towers, where sterility breeds contempt for the street.

Architecture defined as "commodity, as speculative object, as instrument of ideology" was meant by Benjamin to be a prognosis of the ills afflicting the architecture of the late nineteenth century. It remains a relevant diagnosis today. After all, are the millions of square feet in recently created office space anything more than naked speculation? The Renaissance defined commodity from the Medieval Latin "commodiosus": spacious, roomy, convenient, suitable. We define it "...as anything useful that can be turned to commercial advantage." And, seer that he was, Benjamin could not have anticipated the replacement of political by corporate ideologies, the replacement of the state architectures of the French Empire and Bismarck's Prussia, of Mussolini's Italy and the excesses of the Third Reich. They have literally and figuratively been overshadowed by the no less ideological architectures of IBM and AT&T.

In point of fact this essay is not concerned with future forebodings or the mourning for a lost past; it is about present opportunities and civic self-interest. From the viewpoint of urban planning, Jacobs has taught us that we desperately need a "close-grained" stock of aged but reputable structures to promote the city's continued economic health. "As for really new ideas of any kind—no matter how ultimately profitable or otherwise successful some of them might prove to be—there is no leeway for such chancy trial, error and experimentation in the high-powered economy of new construction. Old ideas can sometimes use new buildings. New ideas must use old buildings."

Economic considerations, however, are an abstraction out on the street. We are touched instead by the evidence of our senses, by the color and texture of the environment, by its ability to amuse us, console us, teach us. Primordial art, consciously or not, begins by imitation, and slowly matures into synthesis and self-realization. Our terra-cotta heritage, marked as it is by the eclectic gathering of influences from the Middle Ages onward, is one of our principal learning tools. By such means do we educate ourselves. From such alphabet blocks comes the language of architecture.

Payne Apartments *(cat. 51)*
A. Warren Gould, Architect, c. 1914
Old ideas can sometimes use new buildings, new ideas must use old buildings.

Josephinum *(cat. 102)*
Eames and Young, Architects, c. 1906
These imitations in terra-cotta of details from the Italian masters are Seattle's first grappling with "aesthetic consumerism," our first faltering step towards the city as a work of art.

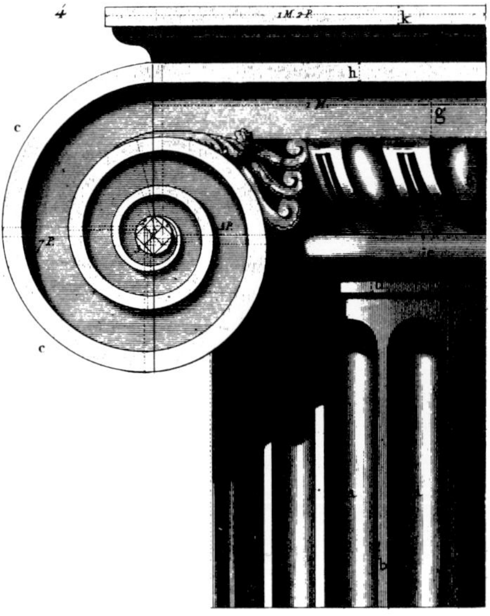

Volute

Acanthus

A plant with thick, fleshy scalloped leaves used on Corinthian and on Composite capitals and other moldings. According to Vitruvius, the acanthus leaf ornament was invented when "A girl, a native of Corinth, already of age to be married, was attacked by disease and died. After her funeral, the goblets which delighted her when living were put into a basket by her nurse and placed at the top of the monument. That they might remain longer, exposed as they were to the weather, she covered the basket with a tile.

As it happened the basket was placed on the root of an acathus. In spring the plant shoots grew up the sides of the basket and being pressed down at the angles by the force of the weight of the tile, were compelled to form the curves of volutes at the extreme parts. Then Callimachus, who for the elegance and refinement of his marble carving was nicknamed catatechnos by the Athenians, was passing the monument, and perceived the basket and the young leaves growing up. Pleased with the style and novelty of the grouping, he made the columns for the Corinthians on this model and fixed the proportions…." Whatever the truth of this anecdote, the deeply cut and symmetrical leaves of the acanthus were first stylized and used by the Greeks.

Acroterias

Plinths for statues or ornaments placed at the apex and ends of a pediment; also, more loosely, both the plinths and what stands on them.

Anthemion

From the Greek for a cluster of flowers, the term describes a fan-shaped floral ornament commonly held to be a

stylized honeysuckle blossom. Anthemia were ubiquitous in Classical Greece, from painted bands on vases to antefixae and friezes on temples.

Antefix, Antefixae

Initially the ornamental blocks placed at the edges of the tiles on the roofs of the Greek temples, the term now refers to any similar ornament on the cornice of a building. Antefixae were most often in the shape of an anthemion.

Arabesque

Complex curled spirals interwoven into overlaid zigzags and other geometric shapes too intricate and complex for easy comprehension. The first such designs were actually Roman but the name derives from the great use of such patterns in Islamic architecture—due in great part to Koranic prohibitions regarding graven images. Indeed, many Islamic arabesques are quotations of the Koran in highly stylized and ornamented calligraphy.

Baluster, Balustrade

A baluster is a short post or pillar, often vase shaped, supporting a rail or coping and thus forming a balustrade. The word bal-

uster derives from the Italian for the flower of the wild pomegranate, the double curved flower which the baluster is said to resemble. Bannister, incidentally, is a corruption of baluster.

Bracket

In classical orders, a small stone beam of rectangular shape set in series to support a cornice. When set with the length along a vertical axis in the shape of an S-curled double

scroll with the larger curl to the top, a bracket is called a console. The same shape extending horizontally and covered with an acanthus leaf is called a modillion.

Bucranium
The Greeks placed necklaces of flowered garlands on the oxen they led to sacrifice. These garlands were draped

between the skulls of such oxen sacrificed, and on the sides of the altars. Later, these garlands became ornamental carvings on temple friezes. By the Roman era, this had become an ornament of bulls' heads and festoons in sequence. An excellent example of this ornament is found on the Coliseum Theater.

Cable Molding
An ornament deriving from the style of Romanesque architecture in the form of a molding resembling twisted cord or rope.

Cartouche
Heraldry was a symbolic system, a language or writing, whereby a mostly illiterate warrior class distinguished friend from foe by the patterns painted on shields and pennants. With the Renaissance and the spread of courtly man-

ners and learning among a more civilized aristocracy and the merchant class, such coats of arms became the oval shields of noncombatants surrounded by a symbolic parchment of a patent of nobility. The word is from the French, and first meant a rolled cone of paper containing groceries or a charge of gunpowder for a muzzle-loading gun. Later, the term was extended to mean any oval shape in a scrolled frame. To compound the confusion, archeologists in the Napoleonic era applied the term to the oval insignia of the pharoahs and high-born Egyptians.

Chevron
Deriving or at least related to the plural of

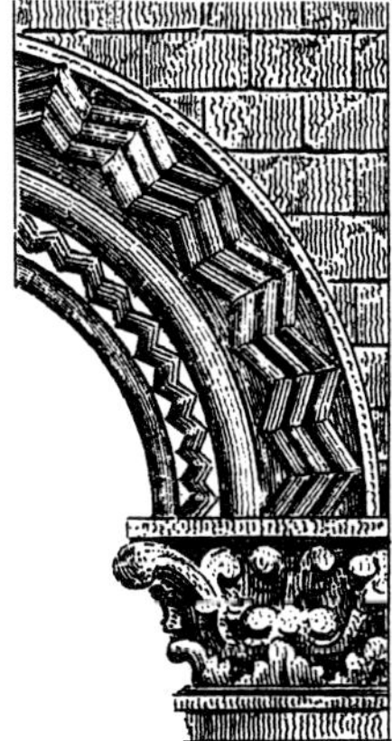

the Latin diminutive for goat, the term originally meant the meeting of two rafters in a point at an upwards angle—perhaps like two rams or buck goats butting heads. As decoration, a heraldic convention of a zigzag pattern of linked Vs banding across an escutchion and later an architectural molding originated in the Romanesque style.

Cladding
A veneer of stone or any other appropriate material applied to a building as frosting to a cake. Cladding was first used extensively by the Romans, who built massive structures replete with arches and, often, domes, covering them with a skin of marble or stucco ornamented with moldings and pilasters derived from the columns, capitals and entablatures of the five orders. More germane to our study is the terra-cotta cladding hung from brick or steel on downtown office buildings and hotels built in the earliest decades of this century. The ornament of this cladding comes from the styles of Gothic, Romanesque and Art Deco architecture, as well as the classical orders.

Console
A bracket, either supporting a cornice or freestanding and purely ornamental, in the form of an S-curled scroll of uneven proportions, usually aligned along the vertical with the larger curl to the top.

Cornice
Initially the uppermost—and outermost—member of an entablature of one of the established orders of classical architecture and now more commonly referring to any similar horizontal molding crowning or overhanging the top of a building.

Dentil, Dentils
A series of small rectangular blocks set somewhat apart in rows on cornices of the classical orders in order to

create bands of light and shadow and, hence, any similar ornament on later buildings.

Egg-and-Dart
An ancient Greek ornamental motif—also called echinus or sea

urchin—of points and pointed ovals or eggs and arrowheads or similar projectile points in alternation. Dentils and egg-and-dart moldings are commonplace in the terra-cotta ornamentation of the Seattle buildings surveyed in this study.

Entablature
The lintel part of the post-and-lintel construction of the Greek orders, an entablature is the horizontal member above column and capital. Classical entablatures were divided into three bands: the architrave at the bottom, the frieze in the center and the cornice at the top. Ornament and proportions were governed by strict conventions, the same conventions applying to the shape and size of capital and column.

Festoon
A carved or cast ornament representing a curved garland of flowers, fruit and leaves tied up with ribbons and hung between two supports. Yet another ornament ultimately deriving from a religious rite. The word festoon derives from the same root as "festival."

Fleuron
A decorative carved flower or leaf.

Frieze
In the classical orders, the middle division of an entablature, between the architrave and cornice, often carved or decorated, hence, any band of carved or cast ornamentation on the side of a building.

Gargoyle
Originally a water spout in the form of an animal head with the water issuing from the mouth, which derives from the Old French word for throat, as does the English word "gargle." More loosely, it refers to any similar ornament resem-

bling an animal or monstrous head.

Grotesque
A fanciful ornamental decoration blending animal and human features. It was first employed in under-

ground Roman grottoes, hence the derivation of the word. More loosely it refers to any architectural ornament displaying such fantastic qualities.

Guilloche
An enriched molding in the form of a woven plait of interlaced bands.

Modillion
Small brackets spaced in series under the cornices of Corinthian and Composite entablature. When square in shape, they are called mutules.

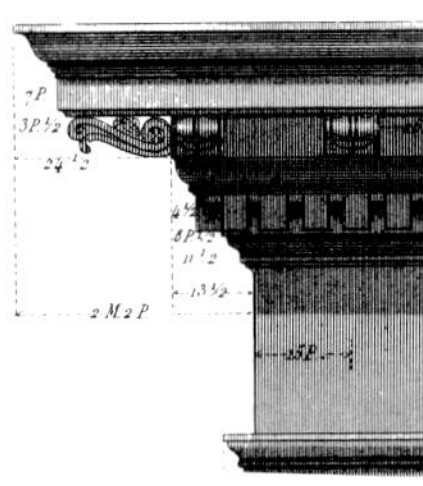

In the Corinthian order, they take the form of consoles extending horizontally with carved acanthus leaves spreading underneath.

Niche
Deriving from the Italian for sea shell, a shallow recess often arched to a Gothic point and set in a wall, sometimes

empty, sometimes holding a vase or an urn, a statue or trophy.

Order
A set of rules governing the size, shape, relative proportions and amount of decoration of an entire column, from base through shaft to capital and entablature. The Greeks knew three: the Doric, the Ionic and the Corinthian, but used mainly the first two — the Corinthian becoming popular in the post-Alexandrian era. The Romans recognized five orders, adding Ionic to Corinthian to produce the Composite and recognizing a variant of the Doric with a smooth unfluted column known as the Tuscan order.

Palmette
A floral ornament in the form of a stylized palm leaf.

Patera
A small circular ornament in the form of a stylized flower.

Pier
A perpendicular masonry support, often upholding an arch; more commonly, the solid wall between doors or windows and sometimes referring to the pillars — not columns — of medieval architectural styles.

Pilaster
A shallow pier or rectangular column projecting only slightly from a wall, often conforming

with one of the five classical orders.

Quoins
From the French for corners, dressed stones or cast terra-cotta bricks laid at the corners of

buildings so that the faces are alternately large and small.

Rinceau
A spiral motif of scrolled vines or acanthus leaves.

Scallop
An ornament resembling a shell.

Scroll
Books in Greek times were written on one continuous length of paper with wooden handles often attached at either end. To read, one merely kept rolling such a scroll, as they were called, from handle to handle. In architecture, the representation of a partially unrolled scroll, such as the volute of an Ionic capital.

Strapwork
An architectural decoration resembling cut leather worked in interlaced bands.

Swag
Draped cloth expressed in stone or terra-cotta, hung from an urn or as a festoon suspended between two supports.

Tracery
Originally, the ornamental intersections in the upper parts of windows, screens and panels in Gothic and Romanesque architecture and, hence, the decorative use of these on blank walls and false gables.

Volute
A spiral scroll on an Ionic capital and ornaments derived from this form.

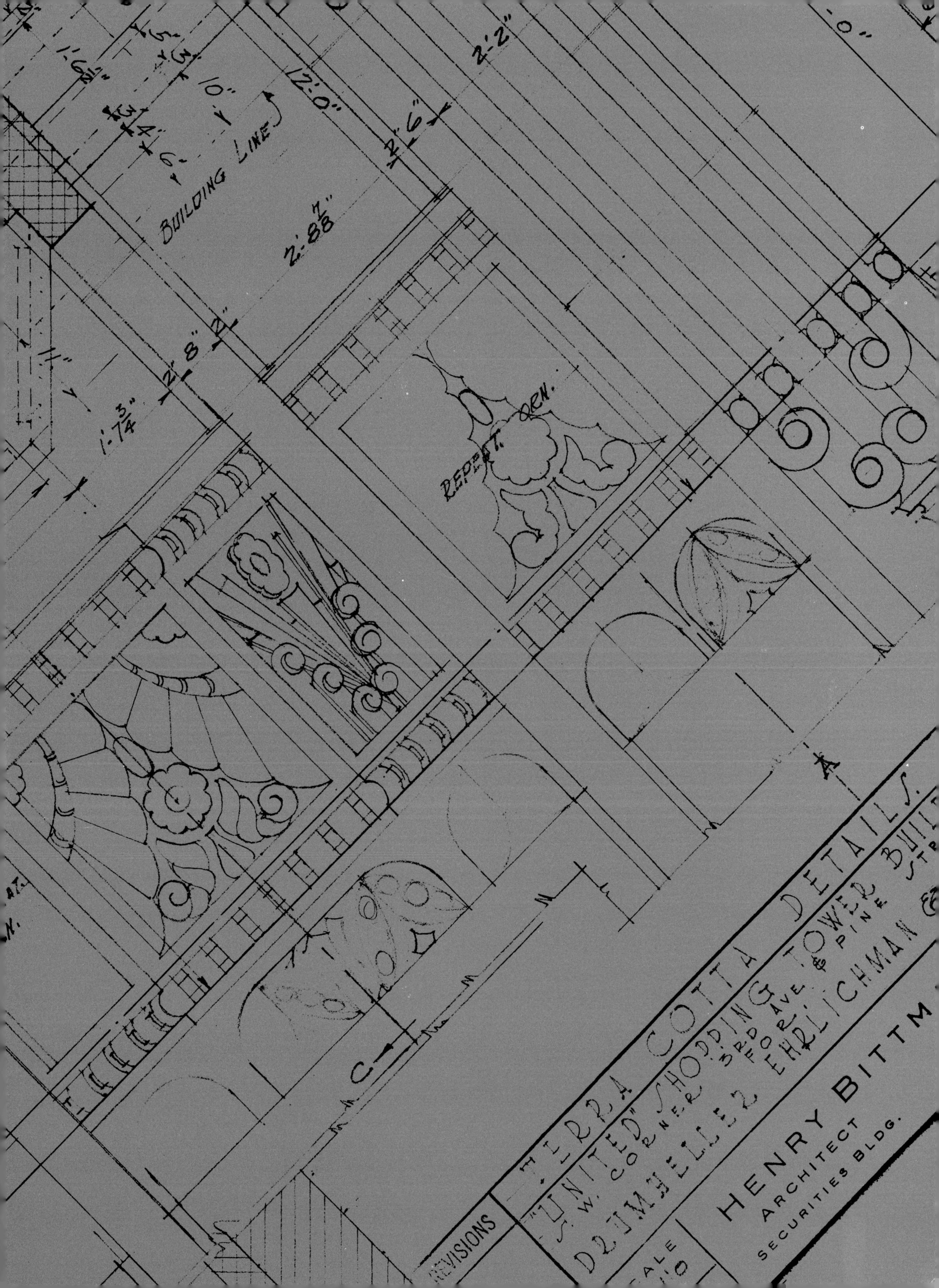

BUILDING LINE
12'-0"
2'-2"
2'-6"
2'-8 7/8"
2'-8"
1'-7 3/4"
REPEAT ORN.
A
C
TERRA COTTA DETAILS.
"UNITED" SHOPPING TOWER
S. W. CORNER 3RD AVE. & PINE
FOR
DRUMHELLER & EHRLICHMAN
HENRY
ARCHITECT
SECURITIES BLDG.
REVISIONS

The Building Catalogue

The following inventory represents an attempt to catalogue all buildings clad or ornamented with terra-cotta that are existing in downtown Seattle as of the date of this publication. Information is presented in the following order:

Contemporary name of building
(Historic name, if known, or if different)
Address
Date of construction (Where two dates are given, sources of information differed. The dates probably represent date of building permit or construction commencement, and date of completion.)
Designer or design firm

While we believe this is a comprehensive catalogue of downtown Seattle's terra-cotta architecture, we do not assert that it is without errors of omission or misidentification. The bulk of the inventory was compiled from visual identification of the buildings. Since one of the features of terra-cotta is its ability to mimic other materials, positive identification is often challenging.

1.
North Coast Importing Company
(Freedman Building)
515 Maynard Avenue S.

2.
Rainier Heat and Power Company
650 S. Jackson Street

3.
514 S. Jackson Street
1916
J.C. McCanby

4.
Downtowner Apartments
(New Richmond Hotel)
308 Fourth Avenue S.
1911/1912
Gould & Champney

5.
Frye Apartments
(Frye Hotel)
223 Yesler Way
1911
Bebb & Mendel

6.
City Club Building
112 First Avenue S.
1897/1905

7.
Delmar Building
(Delmar Hotel)
114-116 First Avenue S.
1890
H. Steinman

8.
Seattle Quilt Building
(Walker Building)
318 First Avenue S.
1904
Boone & Corner

9.
Terry-Denny Building
109-115 First Avenue S.
1893

10.
Merrill Place
(Schwabacher Hardware)
First Avenue S. & Jackson Street
1905
Bebb & Mendel

11.
Young Womens' Christian Association
Fifth Avenue & Seneca Street
1913
Champney & Gould

12.
First United Methodist Church
811 Fifth Avenue
1907/1910
Shack & Huntington

13.
Olympic Hotel[2]
410 Seneca Street
1923/1929
George B. Post & Sons; Bebb & Gould

14.
(Fourth Avenue Hotel)
406-410 Fourth Avenue
1905
Wilcox

15.
Old National Bank Building
1119-1125 Fourth Avenue
1922
Henry James

16.
Seattle Hotel
(Earl Hotel)
315 Seneca Street
1928
V.W. Voorhees

17.
Pacific Hotel
(Pembrook Hotel)
317 Marion Street
1915
Wilcox & Everett

18.
Seattle Tower[1,2]
(Northern Life Tower)
1218 Third Avenue
1929
A.H. Albertson; Wilson; P.D. Richards

19.
Telephone Building
1204 Third Avenue
1920
Bebb & Gould

20.
Central Building
810 Third Avenue
1907
C.R. Aldrich

21.
Arctic Club[2]
306 Cherry Street
1914/1917
A. Warren Gould

22.
St. Charles Hotel
619 Third Avenue
1911
John Graham Sr.

23.
Rainier National Bank
(Baillargeon Department Store)
1100 Second Avenue
1908
J.J. Baillargeon

24.
Dexter Horton Building
710 Second Avenue
1922
John Graham Sr.

25.
Alaska Building
618 Second Avenue
1904
Eames & Young

26.
Corona Hotel
(Oriental Building)
608 Second Avenue
1903
Bebb & Mendel

27.
Smith Tower
506 Second Avenue
1912
Gaggin & Gaggin

28.
New Federal Building Plaza
(Burke Building)
920 Second Avenue
1890
Elmer Fisher

29.
Savings Bank of Puget Sound
(Bank of California Building)
815 Second Avenue
1908/1909
John Graham Sr.

30.
Hoge Building Annex
711 Second Avenue
1937
Bebb & Gould

31.
Hoge Building
705 Second Avenue
1911
Bebb & Mendel

32.
Lowman Building
107 Cherry Street
1905
Heide & deNeuf

33.
Lowman & Hanford Building
616 First Avenue
1890

34.
Pioneer Building[2]
606 First Avenue
1889/1892
Elmer Fisher

35.
Watermark Tower
(Coleman Building)
(Puget Mill Company)
First Avenue & Spring Street
1924
Bebb & Gould

36.
Arlington Building[1,2]
(Colonial Building)
1119-1123 First Avenue
1901
Max Umbrecht

37.
Alexis Hotel[1,2]
(Globe Building)
1001-1011 First Avenue
1901
Max Umbrecht

38.
Old Federal Building
(Federal Building)
First Avenue & Madison Street
1932
J.A. Whetmore

39.
McClary-Edenholm Building
625 First Avenue

40.
Mutual Life Building
605 First Avenue
1897/1904
Robertson & Blackwell

41.
Paramount Theater[1]
901 Pine Street
1926
B. Marcus Priteca; Peters

42.
Camlin Hotel
1619 Ninth Avenue
1926
Carl J. Linde

43.
Pande Cameron Building
815 Pine Street
1928
Henry Bittman

44.
Cullen Company Building
1624-1634 Eighth Avenue
1920
John Graham Sr.

45.
Nootka Investment Company
(demolished 1985)
715 Pike Street
1925
John Graham Sr.

46.
McKay Apartment Hotel
711 Pike Street
1914
John Graham Sr.

47.
Eagles Auditorium & Theater [1,2]
1404 Seventh Avenue
1924/1925
Henry Bittman

48.
Hubbel Building
(slated for demolition)
704 Union Street
1922
Henry Bittman

49.
Tower Building
(Textile Tower Building)
1813 Seventh Avenue
1930
Earl W. Morrison

50.
Roosevelt Hotel
Seventh Avenue & Pine Street
1929/1930
John Graham Sr.

51.
Payne Apartments
1521 Seventh Avenue
1914
A. Warren Gould

52.
Lloyd Building
601-611 Stewart Street
1925
V.W. Voorhees

53.
Seattle Trust Building
(Times Square Garage)
Sixth Avenue & Olive Way
1925
Stoddard & Son

54.
Klopfenstein's
(Post-Intelligencer Building)
600 Pine Street
1920
John Graham Sr.

55.
Medical-Dental Building
(Medical Arts Building)
505 Olive Way
1925
Kreutzer & Albertson; John Graham Sr.

58.
Washington Athletic Club
1325 Sixth Avenue
1930
Sherwood D. Ford

61.
Nordstrom Department Store,
south end
(Ranke Building)
1501 Fifth Avenue
1926
Louis Svarz

56.
Sixth & Pine Building[2]
(Shafer Building)
515 Pine Street
1923/1924
Joseph E. Blackwell

59.
Frederick & Nelson
Department Store
500 Pine Street
1919
John Graham Sr.

62.
Times Square Building[1,2]
414 Olive Way
1915
Bebb & Gould

57.
Decatur Building[1]
(Grunbaum Building)
1521 Sixth Avenue
1921
Henry Bittman

60.
Coliseum Theater[1,2]
1506 Fifth Avenue
1916
B. Marcus Priteca

63.
Mayflower Park Hotel
(The Bergonian)
1630 Fourth Avenue
1927
Stuart Wheatley

64.
Seaboard Building
(Northern Securities Building)
1506 Westlake Avenue
1906/1909
W.D. Van Siclen

65.
Fourth & Pike Building
(Ligget Building)
1424 Fourth Avenue
1926
Lawton & Moldenhour

66.
Joshua Green Building
1425 Fourth Avenue
1913
John Graham Sr.

67.
Fourth Avenue Building
(Equitable Building)
1417 Fourth Avenue
1920
A. Wheatley

68.
Cobb Building
(White Building)
1307 Fourth Avenue
1909
Howells & Stokes

69.
Woolworth's Store
301 Pike Street
1939
Harold B. Hamhill

70.
Vance Building
(Joseph Vance Building)
1402 Third Avenue
1929
V.W. Voorhees; John Graham Sr.

71.
Olympic Tower[2]
(United Shopping Tower)
217 Pine Street
1929
Henry Bittman

72.
Fischer Studio Building
(Fischer Music Studio)
1519 Third Avenue
1912/1915
Bebb & Mendel; Bebb & Gould

73.
Melbourne House
(Republic Building)
1511 Third Avenue
1927
Lawton & Moldenhour

74.
Kress Building
(Kress Variety Store)
1423 Third Avenue
1923
E.J. Hoffman, New York

75.
Mann Building[2]
1401 Third Avenue
1926
Henry Bittman; Sherwood Ford

76.
Air Force Reserve Offices
(Shorett & Riely Building)
1623 Second Avenue
1914
Charles Bebb

77.
Doyle Building
(J.S. Graham Department Store)
1527 Second Avenue
1919
A.E. Doyle; Merriam

78.
Second & Pike Building
(Eitel Building)
1507 Second Avenue
1908
W.D. Van Siclin

79.
Metropolitan Health Club
114 Pike St.
1922
Pierre Horrocks & J.C. Nevin

80.
York Lunch
1500 First Avenue
1924
J. Lister Holmes

81.
Fantasy Limited
(Broderick Building)
1504 First Avenue
1922
John Graham Sr.

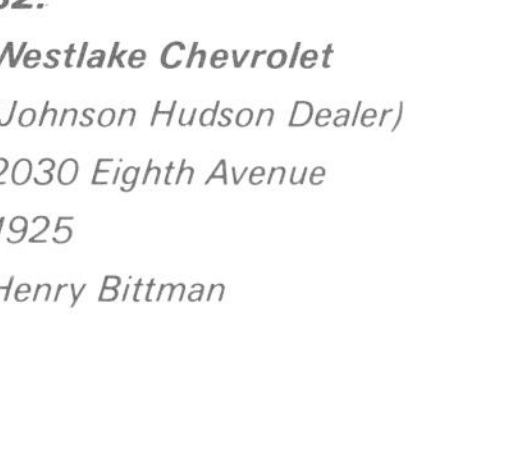

82.
Westlake Chevrolet
(Johnson Hudson Dealer)
2030 Eighth Avenue
1925
Henry Bittman

83.
(Craftsman Press)
2030 Westlake Avenue
Henry Bittman

84.
(Westlake Hotel)
2004 Westlake Avenue

85.
Vance Hotel
620 Stewart Street
1926
V.W. Voorhees

86.
Kongsli's Fifth Avenue Court
2132 Fifth Avenue

87.
Sheridan Apartments
(William D. Perkins Building)
2011 Fifth Avenue
1915/1928
David Dow; J.A. Crautzer

88.
Griffin Business College
(Wilson Institute)
2005 Fifth Avenue
1927
Frank H. Fowler

89.
Superior Reprographics
(G.M. Bell Building)
1923 Fifth Avenue
1911/1915
David Dow

90.
Franklin Apartments
2302 Fourth Avenue
1918
Lawton & Moldenhour

91.
Centennial Building
(Tyee Investment Company Building)
1904 Fourth Avenue
1925
Henry Bittman

92.
Fleming Apartments
2321 Fourth Avenue
1916/1918
Warren Milner

93.
(Hotel Lorraine)
2213-2217 Fourth Avenue
1916
Warren Milner

94.
Adams Apartments
304-308 Bell Street
1915
V.W. Voorhees

95.
Cornelius Hotel Apartments
306 Blanchard Street

96.
Securities Building
(Washington Securities Building)
1904 Third Avenue
1912/1915
John Graham Sr.; Frank Allen

97.
Downtown Mini-Warehouse
(Grimshaw Garage)
1915 Third Avenue
1928
Henry Bittman

98.
Peoples National Bank Building
(Scott Building)
1907 Third Avenue
1921
Charles Haynes

99.
Castle Apartments
2132 Second Avenue
1918
E.W. Lawton

100.
Palladian Apartments
(Calhoun Hotel)
2000 Second Avenue
1909/1910
W.R. White

101.
Moore Egyptian Theater[2]
(Moore Theater & Hotel)
1932 Second Avenue
1907/1908
E.W. Houghton

102.
The Josephinum
(New Washington Hotel)
1902 Second Avenue
1906
Eames & Young

103.
McGraw Kittinger & Case, Inc.
2331 Second Avenue

104.
William Tell Hotel
2327 Second Avenue
1924
J. Lister Holmes

105.
The Humphrey
2205 Second Avenue
1923
Warren Milner

106.
Rivoli Apartments
2125-2129 Second Avenue
1909
Howell & Stokes

107.
Bethel Pentecostal Temple
(The Natatorium)
2019-2035 Second Avenue
1915
B. Marcus Priteca

108.
Merchandise Mart
(Puget Sound News Building)
1931 Second Avenue
1915
Bebb & Gould

109.
Austin A. Bell Building
(Bell Apartments)
2324 First Avenue
1889
Elmer Fisher

110.
Terminal Sales Building
1932 First Avenue
1923
Henry Bittman

111.
Oxford Apartments
(Hotel Oxford)
1920 First Avenue
1909
Frank Allen Inc.

112.
Continental Furniture Warehouse
(Union Stable)
2200 Western Avenue
1909
Benjamin & Maddocks

113.
Olive Tower
1624 Boren Avenue
1928
Earl W. Morrison

114.
Bonair Apartments
1823 Terry Avenue

115.
P.I. Surplus Plus
2403-2419 Second Avenue
1927
Earl W. Morrison

116.
Seattle Firefighters Union
(Cooks & Assistants Union)
2400 First Avenue
1929
Stoddard & Son

117.
The Davenport Apartments
420 Vine Street
1924
Henry Bittman

118.
Labor Temple
2800 First Avenue
1942

119.
Sailors Union of the Pacific
2505 First Avenue
1954
T. Bohannon/K. Better

120.
Film Exchanges
2403 Second Avenue
1927
Earl W. Morrison

[1] *Designated Landmark, National Trust for Historic Preservation.*
[2] *Designated Landmark, City of Seattle Landmarks Preservation Board.*